CAROUSEL
8 DOWN

Decline of the
Canadian Political Brand

Hi Peter
— To a man with much charisma and understanding
— Peter

◆ FriesenPress

Suite 300 - 990 Fort St
Victoria, BC, Canada, V8V 3K2
www.friesenpress.com

Copyright © 2015 by Peter Blaikie
First Edition — 2015

All rights reserved.

No part of this publication may be reproduced in any form, or by any means, electronic or mechanical, including photocopying, recording, or any information browsing, storage, or retrieval system, without permission in writing from FriesenPress.

ISBN
978-1-4602-6896-4 (Hardcover)
978-1-4602-6897-1 (Paperback)
978-1-4602-6898-8 (eBook)

1. Political Science, Political Ideologies, Nationalism

Distributed to the trade by The Ingram Book Company

Table of Contents

Dr. Peter Blaikie — v

Dedication — vii

Chapter 1
Introduction — 1

Chapter 2
Canadian Political Identity — 9

Chapter 3
Multiculturalism: Diversity, Inclusion and the Limits of Tolerance — 22

Chapter 4
The Federal Spending Power — 36

Chapter 5
Institutions — 56

Chapter 6
Intergovernmental Situations — 73

Chapter 7
Federal-Provincial Fiscal Transfer Relations — 91

Chapter 8
Canadian Foreign Policy — 105

Chapter 9
Conclusions — 121

Appendix 1 — 127

Appendix 2 — 133

Notes — 137

Dr. Peter Blaikie

About the author: Dr. Peter Blaikie is a retired professor of Political Science who taught at The University of Alberta and a number of other post-secondary institutions. He also was employed with Alberta Intergovernmental Affairs for many years, specializing on the Constitution, Finance, Health, Education and Human Rights issues.

Dedication

I could not have done this without the sea,
my flowers and the hummingbirds that visit them.

Chapter 1
Introduction

Carousel Eight may be the ultimate embodiment and epitome of who we are as Canadians, or what we should be.[1] It is easy to confuse the two. In early December 2013, West Jet decided to do something very special for their fliers from Toronto and Hamilton en route to Calgary. One passenger after another, bored with the waiting, stood in front of a TV-like machine at the airport with a Santa Claus who asked them what they wanted for Christmas. The children wanted stuffed toys, toy trains, iPods, and so on. One set of haggard parents wanted a big TV, while other adults asked for tickets home for Christmas. Three single women asked for boyfriends! Hey, it is Santa, and the sky is the limit. It was a big, big list indeed.

Well, the West Jet elves got very busy in Calgary to fulfill the requests. They scurried around in a number of stores to find the gifts. Then, needed to wrap and package them. It must have been a logistics nightmare worthy of some kind of military award! The tired passengers arrived in Calgary on time and lined up to get their baggage. But their luggage was not the first thing to come off Carousel Eight. Lo and behold, Christmas boxes spewed forth from this place. And they all had names on them. The stuffed toys, the iPods, the free tickets, even a 50-inch TV all came off of Carousel Eight. The passengers were awed. Not just the children, but the parents and adults as well. Enough tears flowed to wash the airport away!Ok, the three single women might have been disappointed with their Ken dolls, but what was West Jet to do? Bring in the Chippendales?

Of course, this was a major publicity coup for West Jet. At over forty-million hits on YouTube, the airline has probably captured a lot of positive attention from Canadians, Americans, and others, which will likely be a factor for some time when reservations are made. Nonetheless, if this true story brings no tears to your eyes, then you may not be a Canadian.

So what does Carousel Eight tell us about who we are, or are not, as Canadians? What has become of us? Is there an "us"? Canadians are navel gazers; that is the distinguishing characteristic of us as a people. We are incessantly questioning who we are that it seems to be our identity. It is so anathema to the American concept of who they might be: They think they are the most powerful country on earth (true), the most generous people on earth (not true), and are somehow the most exceptional people ever on earth (what does that mean?). "Exceptionalism" is as the deeds it produces and gives way to.[2] They certainly are not exceptional in the two major areas that deplete any country's budget: health and education. Or in a declining reputation in the international political system. But neither is Canada. But this country makes no pretenses; that is difficult to do while contemplating one's navel!

This book outlines and illustrates some of the major areas where we are in trouble as a people politically, economically, and socially. This is no attempt to address all of the major afflictions affecting Canada. Arthritic political atrophy has set in. It may no longer be good enough to engage in the angst of who we are or who we are not. There may be no pills to cure what ails us.

The second chapter is about Canadian political identity. With all of the melding required to put this place together, is it possible to sustain this country over time? The dual English-French beginnings, First Nations Peoples, and the massive influx of immigrants have presumably blended Canadians into some kind of simpatico multi-cultural mix. It is difficult to assess the cultural and political ethos of this country. Sometimes a country is identified by its projects. The railways in Canada are one example. The TransCanada Highway is another. Universal health care, although mainly funded and delivered by the provinces, is yet another. After all, Tommy Douglas, Premier of Saskatchewan and founder of Canadian Health Care, is identified as the most noteworthy citizen this country has ever produced.

Perhaps the intercontinental trails, when completed, could be a new project identifier. With no specific internal vision, and a dearth of new projects, it is difficult to see how a country moves forward as one. Attempting to define Canada in terms of what it is not (Americans) is not an alternative that deserves attention. Chapter three delves into the specifics of multiculturalism. "Social inclusion" is the term used by Prime Minister Harper to emphasize that all immigrants should feel at home in Canada.[3] It is all about celebrating our differences in diversity while integrating newcomers into the social milieu that is called Canada. It is not easy to resolve this process. The "melting pot" concept in the US was always a myth: Immigrants from all over the world do not integrate instantly and cannot be expected to do so. But the problem in Canada is that diversity is encouraged, and partly paid for through federal and provincial programs. The very idea of blending in is quite avoidable for those that wish to do so. What this leads to are enclaves of difference within the Canadian fabric, and this undermines any idea of a oneness within this democracy. Celebration of our differences, which allows different ethnic groups to live in isolation, is politically dysfunctional. It has been said that "miracles can happen if we act as one,"[4] but there is no oneness here. The lightness has turned very grey.

Chapter four addresses issues related to federal spending power. In Canada, this power is virtually unlimited, as interpreted through the Courts. What this power does is allow the federal government to intrude into areas of provincial jurisdiction in which it otherwise has no authority to do so. It is a reality that provinces do not have the fiscal capacity to carry out their constitutional responsibilities. They are dependent on the whims of the federal government to supply the fiscal difference for health and post-secondary education. A separate Equalization Program helps those provinces with less taxation revenues. The current situation is unstable and dysfunctional to the future of the Canadian political system. Ideally, the federal government would transfer the needed tax room to the provinces so that they could provide services to their citizens. This is unlikely to happen, as such a transfer would essentially mean that the federal government would relinquish any say over such major areas as health care. Nonetheless, the current system obfuscates who is responsible for what. Paying functions under the spending power and administrative functions outlined in the Constitution are not transparent, and cause great conflict between the federal and provincial governments. There is a lack of accountability as a consequence, since the payer is not always the same as the administrator.

The fifth chapter is a brief on Canada's political institutions and how they have failed their citizenry. The House of Commons is driven through the Prime Minister and his political appointees in the Prime Minister's Office, and even the Privy Council Office (professional civil service people) has become politicized under this Prime Minister. In a parliamentary system, majority governments are expected to pass legislation with some facility. At the same time, back benchers (those not in Cabinet in the majority party) are supposed to be integral participants in the process. What has happened in Canada is that backbenchers have become yea sayers, reading from speaking notes, puppets on a string. This is not democracy. Major changes have been proposed, but no action has taken place. Omnibus bills are passed in a blink that legislate many disparate items into one overarching bill with no relation to one another. This is called pork barrel legislation in the US, and it is even a declining instrument in Washington with their budget deficit issues. However, in Canada this is authoritarian power, and it is only possible in a system that has no checks and balances under modern majority government.

The problems with the Senate being effectively controlled by the Prime Minister does not bode well for the future of that institution. It is unacceptable that the PMO can define what the Senate will do or will not do; so much for the concept of the Senate being a body of "second sober thought". Its legitimacy has seriously been undermined, and provinces that were once avid supporters of an elected Senate are now balking.

Judicial decisions by the Supreme Court may certainly be mostly correct in many instances, but they have undermined the traditional concept of a parliamentary system which depends on the elected members for its legitimacy. The Constitution Act, 1982, was a change of monolithic proportions in Canadian politics. The Morganthaler decision in 1988 to give women full control over their own bodies relative to abortion is huge.[5] The decision in late 2013 to legalize prostitution is almost mind-boggling, given the conservative bent of the government in power against any such change.[6] Legalizing euthanasia is next on the agenda. And perhaps legalizing marijuana after that. The Courts have taken power over elected members of Parliament because the latter are unwilling to make and take tough decisions for fear of their own electoral prospects. The nine judges on the Supreme Court are indeed supreme. Responsible government requires the Prime Minister and Cabinet to be accountable to Parliament (all MPs) and to its citizens. This role is emaciated and undermined when unelected bodies determine important outcomes in a democracy.

Add in the role of the provinces and territories, and it is no wonder why this country works under severe stresses and strains. Provinces are equal participants in Canadian federalism, and do not accept the very idea of "levels of government," rather than equal orders of government. Is a parliamentary system compatible with a federal system? Is Canada a contradiction in terms in a political sense?

After all, the largest expenses of governments are in health, education, and welfare. And the provinces are responsible for all of them. And this is the problem: the provinces do not have access to the fiscal taxation means to carry out their responsibilities.

Chapter six discusses Intergovernmental Situations. That Quebec never signed onto the Constitution Act, 1982, yet is subject to its provisions, does not bode well for a future for Canada. Attempts through Meech Lake in 1987[7] and the failed Charlottetown referendum in 1992[8] are indicative of a Canada failed. The country muddles through, but there is no élan or common spirit that holds the place together. Alberta and BC Cabinets have met on several occasions to finalize their own bilateral relations related to accreditation, trucking regulations, etc. There is still no single authority for the regulation of securities in Canada.

As the federal government has shied from any formative role in the past seven years, the provinces have been filling the vacuum. Politics within the provinces will always be an issue with the potential to undermine interprovincial agreement. Even for Alberta and BC, which both share conservative style governments, agreements on a pipeline to move oil from Fort McMurray to the west coast are stalled. That Quebec is unwilling to allow a new hydroelectric network to move from Newfoundland through its territory is a powerful reminder of the power of localized provincial politics. And alternatives are there as the lines will be run under the water through to Nova Scotia and New Brunswick with federal assistance, to which Quebec objects.

It is no longer possible for Canadians to define themselves by what they are not: Americans. With federal-provincial relations perpetually on the skids, and the politics of individual provinces in flux, it is difficult to see how Canada moves forward as a federal state. Dysfunction seems to be the only constant.

Fiscal transfers are the subject of chapter seven. This chapter details the significant amounts of money that are transferred from the federal government to the provinces. It also discusses the acrimony in federal-provincial relations resulting from unilateral federal decisions and a general lack of communication between the two sets of governments, particularly over the past seven years. Over $62 billion will be transferred in 2013-2014 from the federal government, yet it is a paltry number in comparison to what provinces spend in health, education, and social services, far and away the major areas of provincial spending. It is important to note that as established in 1977, the federal government was in for 50% of such expenditures. The federal erosion in spending began in 1982 and has continued ever since. The current federal-provincial-territorial fiscal transfer system is haphazard, uncooperative and destined to create continuing strife among jurisdictions. It is on a very sharp cliff.

The problems in the system are numerous: 1) There is no transparency; 2) There is no accountability; 3) There are no negotiations anymore; 4) There is no attempt to address fiscal imbalances between its revenues and the lack of revenues of most provincial governments. There is also the issue of horizontal imbalances, since a few provinces have much more fiscal capacity and taxing capabilities than the rest. The conundrum is which provinces are over or under compensated, and how can these matters be addressed and resolved.

Canadian foreign policy is the subject of chapter eight. It illustrates a massive departure from past governments in only seven years. A new unilateralism has been the philosophy of the Harper Government. A move away from involvement in UN agencies is part of it. And withdrawal from environmental accords and desertification, as well as a backing away from participation in key non-governmental organizations has also become part of the new mantra. A narrow, myopic vision of the Middle-East, including staunch support for all Israeli positions and opposition to a Palestinian state, and diplomatic withdrawal from Iran are not consistent with past foreign policies in this country.

To the extent that a country's identity is mirrored in how others see it, Canada is in very deep trouble. Not securing a seat on the UN Security Council is indicative of what others think of Canada. There can be no denial. Canada has gone into its shell in regards to foreign relations, and that explains why the Prime Minister refuses to address the General Assembly on an annual basis. All of this speaks to the dysfunction within the Union of Canada.

The final chapter summarizes the issues that have been detailed in this book. It is difficult to see how Canada moves forward without vision, without projects, with strained federal-provincial relations, and sometimes interprovincial relations as well. Depending on Courts to resolve all important issues for the country is problematic and undemocratic.

Two appendixes are attached to the text. The first is about the Mayor Ford debacle in Toronto, its connection to Harper, and its possible meaning for Canada. The second outlines an insidious example of cooperation between the Government of Canada and BC to take away tax refunds, tax credits and possibly other benefits from those not paying healthcare premiums to the province. If this is bilateral cooperation, then this country is in a very sorry state when the federal government is playing handmaiden to a province for ideological and political reasons. In fact, every important decision in Ottawa seems to involve Machiavellian considerations, whether domestic or international. Where is the vision? Where is the humanism?

Carousel Eight is no longer part of the Canadian dream; it is indeed Canada lost. A common identity cannot be discerned. Federal-provincial and intergovernmental relations are in a state of crisis. Canadian foreign policy is no longer a contributing factor to an "us". The Carousel may still go round and round, but no one is paying any attention. A nation of givers and beneficence has been replaced with a country of doubters and uncharacteristic diffidence and indifference.

Chapter 2
Canadian Political Identity

Introduction:

A political ethos, or a sense of common identity, is essential to sustaining a state over time. The United Kingdom has the Queen; the U.S. has its sense of world hegemony; Russia is trying to identify as something not Eastern or Western.China has always seen itself as the centre. Congruous and harmonious beliefs, aspirations, dreams and objectives are all essential to political, economic, and social system survival. Does the very composition of Canadian political society contribute to such an ethos, or undermine it? Was this nation, from the outset, destined to self-destruct? Are there remedies that could patch the system back together so that Canadians can move forward as one people? These are some of the questions that will be addressed in this chapter.

Political identity can be defined as, "...the way in which citizens situate themselves in relation to the world around them, which includes political institutions... political communities... and fellow citizens as members of a shared community."[1] To have a common political identity, citizens in Canada would simultaneously have to identify and respect their Ottawa based political institutions as well as their provincial ones. They would support the dual nature of an English and French Canada. They would have to feel a shared political community with those from British Columbia to Newfoundland. They would embrace First Nations Peoples as they carve out their own identities within Canada. They would welcome the multicultural nature of what Canada has become. Is all of this too much to ask? Are the differences so significant that it is an impossible chore to sew them altogether into some kind of grandiose patchwork quilt?

Lewis Carroll's classic, Alice in Wonderland, perfectly characterizes the Canadian nation-state.[2] Somewhere down that rabbit hole, Alice meets the plump, yet regal, caterpillar squatting on that rock, smoking some suspect substance, who blithely blathers, "Whooooooo are youuuuuuu?" This is the state of Canada: Who are Canadians? Canada may be the only country on earth that perpetually, unceasingly engages in contemplative naval gazing. It is a pre-occupation; careers are made out of it!Listen to CBC radio every night!

History:

Uniting Upper and Lower Canada, the English part and the French part, was never going to be an easy task. It was certainly made more complicated by the huge influx of English Loyalists from America in 1776 and afterwards. Thousands upon thousands moved north, and while, by today's demographics, such numbers seem small, they would perhaps equate into hundreds of thousands today, if not millions. The influx was significant enough to change the dynamic of the original English and French populations, and this is poignant. The French nation instantly became a minority nation relative to the English nation. Majority numbers in Upper Canada would certainly etch the content of the Constitution Act 1867, while attempting to provide enough room for provincial and local matters in Quebec and the Maritime joiners. The seeds of suspicion and consternation were certainly built into the fabric of what would become Confederation in 1867.

The Quebec nation was anxious to ensure that its language, culture, religion and unique Napoleonic code (civil code), in distinction to the English common law, would be protected and encouraged in the new union. A more decentralized notion of confederation would help to realize these characteristics of the nation. Ontario and the English nation leaders were leaning more toward a centralized conception of the country, and this was certainly the view of the first Prime Minister in Canada, John A. MacDonald. Right from the outset, then, there were two entirely distinct and contradictory notions of what it would mean to be a Canadian. Developing a nation-state based on contradictions is not a good start to nation-building.

Trying to integrate two entirely different cultures into a political entity would be difficult enough. But trying to build a country out of fear is even more problematic. The chapter on Institutions notes the strength of the US in the aftermath of the Civil War (1861-65) and the very real possibility of invasion. Uniting Canada from coast to coast would, according to the Founders, assuage such concerns. The national railroads and high protective tariffs against American imports were seen as unifying forces that would tie this vast land together by encouraging east-west trade. Promises of land in the West drew masses of immigrants from Europe and elsewhere and this certainly augmented the conception that Canada could become a powerful country in its own right, an offset to the elephant to the South. Canada would become a national, showcase dream, every bit as viable as America and its immigrants who landed at Ellis Island in New York and Angel Island in San Francisco.

Thus far, two "un-uniting" anomalous factors have been identified in terms of bringing together Canadians as one people; 1, the dual cultures of English and Quebec; and 2, the fallacious notion that countries can be built, sustained and grown over time through intimidating external threats of invasion. A third issue which has severely undermined Canadian political identity is the impact on the West of decisions made in Ottawa. The high tariffs, which forced Westerners to buy finished products and groceries such as Massey Ferguson tractors and cheese and tinned goods etc., from the East, rather than the US, has certainly contributed to the general malaise, irritation, and lack of a unified political identity.

The historical context is important in determining who a people are, or who they may not be. It imprints the myths and realities of various regions of Canada and is pervasive from generation to generation. Perhaps countries are partly built upon myths, but realities cannot be ignored; atrophy is the result.

Who Are We?

Who are you? Who are we? What is being suggested in this chapter is that there is no "we". Compare a few other countries to elucidate their conceptions of statehood. The US citizenry have no problem identifying who they are: the greatest country on earth, the most powerful country, the god blessed country all want to come to, an exceptional nation like no other. Although this political ethos and identity is significantly based on fabrication and myth, it is held firmly and absolutely; nothing could undermine it. In China, the concept of the eternal middle kingdom, where surrounding nations would forever need to pay due respect and tribute, is firmly entrenched in their ideology. Their drive to challenge the US in economic and military superiority is part of an ethos to overtake. Britain has its historic political institutions and Shakespeare et al. and wry humour to define itself, to which we all owe a debt. Its imperial hegemony over most continents was a unifying factor internally. German industriousness and a persistent sense of nationalism have contributed to its concept of political self.One could go on and on about France, Italy, Japan etc. They know who they are. Who are we?

Canadians are quite good at defining themselves by what they are not. They confidently and haughtily claim that, well, they are not Americans. Even if this were true, which is certainly debatable given the historical backgrounds of both populations, travel, net-dating, inter-marriages, trade relations, and deep affinity amongst the citizenry of both countries and so on, it is a very poor and specious basis to claim a political identity status. Finns do not identify themselves as non-Russian! Sometimes Canadians self-identify as a kinder, gentler version of their American compatriots, a claim which would require substantiation and still begs the question of who Canadians are. If we cannot be something that we are not, then who are we?

In one recent poll, Canadians overwhelmingly chose Tommy Douglas as their national idol.[3] He brought universal health care to Saskatchewan and, ultimately, all of Canada followed suit by 1968. Can one social attribute or program define the political ethos of a country? Certainly, no other nation-state has ever defined itself in these terms. The Swiss are the Swiss, the Brazilians are Brazilians, and Filipinos are Filipinos. Canadians are health care? Defining itself through one social program, which is delivered separately, and sometimes inequitably, in each provincial and territorial jurisdiction is passing strange and does not contribute to any sense whatsoever of a nation-wide political identity. Health care will not do as a means of identifying and defining Canadian identity.

Perhaps symbols can be a source of political identity. Americans are certainly aware of one of their important symbols, the Bald Eagle. In one talon is an olive branch, several arrows in the other. This is a country that perceives itself as keeper of peace in the world and simultaneously as war resolver (or maker). Its national anthem is all about war. Its statue of liberty, sitting in the New York harbour, is a gift from France but is still a potent reminder of American openness toward immigration in the past: Give us your poor, your huddled masses, etc.

Some of Canada's most salient symbols include the following: the Queen, the beaver, maple leaf and RCMP. The problem is that none of them are universally Canadian. For example, the Queen is head of the entire Commonwealth. The beaver is found in many places in North America, even if Canada's first stamp was the three pence beaver in 1851, sixteen years before Confederation! Maple leafs are found all over New England in the US. And no red-leaf Maple trees, producing syrup, survive in Western Canada, except the Manitoba varieties. The maple leaf on the new $20 dollar bill is actually indigenous to Norway.[4] The RCMP is represented nation-wide, but both Ontario and Quebec have their own provincial forces, while rivalries contend for authority between the RCMP and city police forces. Alberta and BC, on occasion, suggest that they will also establish their own provincially based police forces. In any case, it would be perplexing if a country could 'hang its hat' of identity on some perceived symbol of political existence.

A critical part of the political identity problem for Canadian citizens is that they have multiple political affinities: to the nation as a whole, to regions, to provinces and to the very nations from which they came (England, Germany, Italy, China, Japan, the US, etc.). How all of this could be seen as a recipe for coalescence is unimaginable; it is more like a concoction of combined ingredients that has gone very wrong.

Even internally, a province like Quebec may lay claim to being a nation but consider that Quebecers are French, English and Allophone (other immigrants). The latter two significant minorities have been enough thus far to vote down two referenda on separation in 1981 and 1995. French speaking Quebecers on their own would have voted themselves out of Confederation by a significant margin in the mid-55% range in either of those votes. This fact does not bode well for the future of a one Canada concept.

Successive Quebec governments have propagated the concept of dualism to promote the notion of "two nations" in Canada: the English and the French. It is difficult to determine if this is politically motivated or just based on ignorance of the peoples and cultures that exist in English Canada. It is not helpful that even a preponderance of the English speaking political community accepts this idea. It is referred to as ROC (Rest of Canada). ROC is a mythical bird that originated in Madagascar and stories tell that it had talons so strong that it could carry off an elephant.[5] ROC in Canada is as much a political myth in Canada as that ever elusive pink elephant!

Centrifugal Issues

Canadian political identity is impacted by a number of centrifugal forces, militating against a central, national focus; 1, the shear distance of provinces from the central intrastate political institutions in Ottawa; 2, regional identities (the West, the Maritimes, and Ontario, for example); 3, provincial identities; 4, fiscal transfer payments (those receiving more benefits from the federal government are more dependent and may have a closer affinity to the centre than non-dependent provinces[6]; 5, multicultural and First Nations identities; 6,where economics dominates politics.

On late Friday afternoons, intergovernmental high level officials in Alberta in the 1990's mused about their relationship with the federal government in Ottawa. Until the imposition of the National Energy Program in 1980, there was always some faint hope for a semblance of cooperative federalism along the lines of the successfully negotiated Established Programs Financing Act, 1976-77.The rallying call was: How far is Ottawa? Too far away. A nation-wide political ethos and identity still seemed achievable.

The NEP and other related federal measures aimed at confiscating Albertans' wealth, the acrimonious constitutional battles in 1981-82, the introduction of the Goods and Services Tax, and a number of other irritants altered the federal-provincial dynamic for Alberta and some other provinces as well. How far away is Ottawa? Looking east over the Saskatchewan River, the answer was a clarion call: Not nearly far enough.

The Trudeau government was seen as remote from Western provinces and solely concerned with how its policies would impact upon Ontario and Quebec, its major bases of political support. Artificially configuring a low, national Canadian price for oil would surely go over well in the East. After being condemned to being hopeless, world price takers for wheat etc. since entry into Confederation in 1905, now Alberta, BC, and Saskatchewan would be forced to accept losses in oil revenues into the hundreds of billions of dollars.Price takers are those that are forced to what the world markets decide; price makers are those that can manipulate markets and prices like steel, cars etc.

The number of Members of Parliament by province counts in winning elections. In the next election, Ontario and Quebec will have 199 of 338 MP's, or 59%. Can a nation-state really be sustained when the population centres so outnumber the other provinces? Where is the common political identity when the central part dominates the rest? This has certainly been a prime cause of Western Alienation in the West. Important decisions concerning everything from oil pricing to dairy licenses to freight rates etc. are all determined in central Canada. A hodgepodge of attempts has been suggested to reform the Canadian Senate as a means to offset the imbalances in the House of Commons. As concluded in the chapter on Institutions, none of these attempts have been successful and all governments have steered clear of major constitutional reforms in the aftermath of the Meech Lake Accord and Charlottetown failures.

Moreover, it is unclear how some variant of a Triple-E Senate would alleviate alienation in the regions. It would be much more likely to reduce the power of the Premiers and provinces relative to the power centre in Ottawa. This is exactly what has happened in the US, where all political eyes are on Washington D.C., and US Governors have, to a considerable extent, become administrative agents rather than decision-makers in any number of areas.

Political identities in Canada do not necessary coincide with provincial boundaries.[7] Quebec and Ontario may very well self-identify with their province first, and BC and Alberta have sporadically done so usually based on alienating factors. Quebec certainly has a very strong "nationalistic" identity and the Fleur de Lis is an important symbol of this. Ontario identifies itself with its central institutions which are located in Ottawa: Ontario peculiarly thinks of itself as quintessentially Canada.

Regionalism is very important in some areas of the country, particularly the West. But it is quite likely that rural Ontarians share some comparable political and cultural values. The city centres in Alberta,

Edmonton and Calgary, are much more politically similar to their counterparts in BC, Vancouver and Victoria, than they are to their immediate rural riding constituencies, both federally and provincially. The recent election in Alberta speaks to this in obvious ways and is confounding Political Scientists and pundits in Canada and elsewhere.

People living in Western cities share cosmopolitan interests (infrastructure, crime reduction, multicultural integration etc.). Rural communities are more interested in agricultural matters and issues of a local nature. Their populations are less likely to migrate, so a persistence of values transcends generations. Even smaller cities, such as Red Deer, Lethbridge, and Medicine Hat in Alberta, and Kelowna, Penticton, and Chilliwack in BC, share a similar ideology of less government interference in their lives. It is no accident that the nascent Wild Rose Alliance in the 2012 Alberta provincial election did much better in rural areas than in the cities, or that Edmonton managed to elect four NDP members and two Liberals. Even Conservative Calgary elected three Liberals. The same pattern is true in Saskatchewan, where the NDP tends to do better in Regina and Saskatoon than in rural areas.

Regional identities extend beyond provinces which are, after all, artificial creations. Lloydminster, on the border between Alberta and Saskatchewan, demonstrates this perfectly. The political views of the one side and the other are identical. Even more dramatic, perhaps, is that the folks in Cardston, Alberta, definitely share more in common with their northern Montana friends in, say, Kalispell than they do with their own provincial cities. Regional political identity definitely transcends provincial and sometimes international borders. Local, interprovincial and transnational ties all diminish the possibility of a national political identity from shore to shore to shore.

Fiscal transfer payments are also an important motivator in defining political identity. Equalization receiving provinces are much more dependent on Ottawa than those that do not receive such benefits. The Maritimes especially exude more attachment to the political system than those in the three most Western provinces. The reasons why are clear. Dependency creates enduring allegiances. Quebec will always protect its jurisdiction and identity and is not similarly subject to Ottawa's will. Now that Newfoundland is no longer a receiving province, it is likely to take a course in federal-provincial relations that is much closer to that of BC and Alberta than the other Maritime Provinces. None of this bodes well for a single Canadian political identity

Multicultural and First Nations identities are also contributing to a lack of a single political identity in Canada. Canadians typically embrace their differences rather than their similarities: "vive la différence". When RCMP members can wear turbans in recognition of legitimate Sikh religious rites, there are going to be concerns about a one identity Canada. When motorcycle riders claim similar rights, there are serious practical safety and societal issues. France, after all, has banned females wearing Burqas. The courts have not finally determined whether headwear covering a face is legitimate in the voter booth. Clearly, no court would accept such covering if someone was charged with a criminal offense and required a full headshot picture and fingerprint identification.

Multiculturalism celebrates differences. Some of this is very good. Getting to know other cultures, mores etc. is positive and exemplifies a nation welcoming new ideas from throughout the world. Sampling the culinary delights of different places within the confines of your own city is splendid. The downside is that celebrating differences, and offering government support to do so, is not a likely means to contribute to a single political identity. A sense of oneness cannot happen when cocoons of cultural difference are encouraged throughout the land, but principally in the major cities. Envisioned perhaps as a mosaic of peoples living in harmony, the result, especially when state supported, can be political, cultural cacophony. A single national, political identity becomes impossible, and is yet another example of why Canada is not currently viable.

First Nations are claiming their place within the federation. Essentially, until recently, they have been treated as wards of the federal government, products of a series of historical political and judicial decisions gone wrong. Pursuing financial settlements over land claims and rights has now become the ultimate legal cottage industry. First Nations now claim status as an order of government equal to the federal government and provinces. Neither the territories nor cities, the latter of which come under provincial authority, have such status. Some recent Supreme Court decisions have extended aboriginal rights to more extensive consultation regarding such matters as pipelines. The augmented role of First Nations is certainly confusing and bound to create additional strains and dysfunction within the federal system.

Projects

Any country's existence is dependent upon its ability to recreate itself through time. Political system survival requires rejuvenation. There is no better way to do this than through project development. Michael Ignatieff, human rights academic and a former leader of the Liberal Party in Canada, was keenly aware of this basic political tenet.[8] As did others before him, he called for a rapid speed train system that would move from Quebec City to the US border. Alberta premiers have mused about a bullet train between Edmonton and Calgary. Spain already has the bullet trains to speed mobility and windmills galore, as a means to energy sustenance. Such unification measures remain unfulfilled in Canada.

No greater grand visions could be conceived than what the Roosevelt administration did during the US depression in the 1930s. The list is long: The Tennessee Valley Authority (TVA) which provides electricity to many in the South; the Works Program Administration (WPA), which created tens of thousands of jobs and built the Glacier National Park in Montana. There is no more beautiful road in the US than the "going to the sun highway." Necessity breeds creation or re-creation.

China's massive projects overawe all other countries in concepts of revitalization and rediscovery. From the unmatchable fireworks, to freeways that span oceans in Shanghai, there is vision and purpose. This is not to underestimate the critical challenges facing them, including dealing with pollution and opening up their political system to distinct and transparent democratic principles. Rome was not built in a day, yet still died; China is pervasive and enduring. It is the ability to reinvent, adapt and change that energizes.

There is absolutely no indication that Canadian governments have comprehended the concept of re-programming to revitalize, adapt, and move forward as a nation-state. There is no vision. The argument made is that the financial resources do not exist to fund the vision: the piggy bank is busted! This argument is so fallacious it is hardly worthy of a reply. Governments have Herculean powers to borrow and repay. Canadians would gladly buy bonds to support projects that bring pride to their being. The lack of imagination when it comes to creative financing in Canada is quite amazing. It is little solace that Canada's debt to GDP ratio is admirable relative to the rest of the OECD countries if there is no concept or vision of where this country should be headed. A rudderless nation-state is destined to demolition on a shoal of sharp-edged rocks.

Canada is projectless. No vision, no future. Obviously, efforts are being made to realize the Keystone Pipeline to Houston from the oil sands in Fort McMurray. And there are ongoing discussions about moving oil and gas from the West to the East. And, of course, the pipeline to carry oil to Prince Rupert to China and India is all possible. Harsh pro-environmental perspectives do little to create wealth, projects, or anything positive. Is that what Canadians have become: pseudo environmentalists headed for a crash course in cruel economics?

No longer is there a balance between growing the economy and environmental concerns. No compromise. No matter how animated the various interests may be, there seems to be no way to move forward. There is no vision because of the significant and overwhelming divisions within Canadian political society. Jean-Paul Sartre wrote an iconic play, *No Exit*, in the 1940s, which epitomized the human condition as he saw it.[9] It may be even more relevant to Canada than it ever has been. There may be no exit for a nation that has no vision of itself. No state can incessantly define itself by what it is not. Not being American does not a country make.

Chapter 3
Multiculturalism: Diversity, Inclusion and the Limits of Tolerance

1. Introduction

On Thursday, August 29, 2013, Prime Minister Harper stated that, "Our job is social inclusion… making all groups who come to this country, whatever their background, whatever their race, whatever their ethnicity, whatever their religion, feel at home in this country and be Canadians."[1] This is a laudable, lofty comment and is in the tradition of Canadian tolerance. It was made in response to the 2013 proposed Quebec Secular Charter of Rights. There are two key ideas requiring discussion that result from this comment. First, the meaning of "social inclusion" and, second, the definition of "Canadians" as it is used here.

What does social inclusion entail? It implies obligations on the part of the Canadian Government, and perhaps the provinces, as well as visible ethnic immigrants. It also includes the two-nations concept of French and English as well as First Nations Peoples.[2] However, the focus here is on immigrants and not other "nations" currently within our own. Social inclusion must require government to provide a hospitable environment of integration into Canadian society. This could include access to language services and job services, as examples. These are learning tools of inclusiveness and should be embraced; they are definitely not services intended to offer ways of continuing group rights of difference.

To "be Canadian" means to participate in Canadian society: to learn one of the national languages, to vote in elections and to pursue greater objects than one's own cultural, ethnic, or religious heritage. It is, quintessentially, to pursue one's life plan within the Canadian spectrum of possibilities.

The genesis of multiculturalism certainly starts with the Trudeau years.Section 27 of the Charter of Rights and Freedoms, 1982, says: "This Charter shall be interpreted in a manner consistent with the preservation and enhancement of the multicultural heritage of Canadians; they are proud of the fact that Canada is home to many cultural groups." Peter Hogg, a foremost expert on constitutional law in Canada, speculated that S.27 is "more a rhetorical provision than an operative provision"[3]. There have been several Charter of Rights Supreme Court decisions relating to this section as it relates to religious matters, but no cases have reached the Court pertaining to "enhancement" of such rights in any other way. Protection of basic rights to religion are, of course, essential to any democratic society and are the fount of some of the first major immigrations to North America, such as the Plymouth, Massachusetts, pilgrims in 1620, who were persecuted in England.

The Canadian Multiculturalism Act, 1988, C31, is, in fact, a purposeful attempt to go far beyond what was intended in S.27 of the Charter.[4] In S.3(d), it recognizes the existence of communities whose members share a common origin and their development should be enhanced. In S.3(h) we are called upon to foster the appreciation of diverse cultures and to promote the evolving expressions of those cultures. S.5(1) calls on the Minister responsible to project the multicultural reality of Canada in their activities in Canada and abroad. S.5 (h) is to provide support to individuals, groups or organizations to preserve, enhance, and promote multiculturalism. And S.5 (i) encourages the Canadian Government to undertake other projects or programs designed to promote multiculturalism.

Sections 5(h) and S.5(i) of this Act are particularly troublesome as they clearly indicate economic support in favour of multiculturalism: promoting our differences takes priority over what might possibly bind Canadians together. Indeed, the Ministry of Immigration and Multiculturalism has been supporting a number of minorities economically to engage in a multitude of activities and events in support of their heritages. The budget for this area of the department is usually about $21 million, although the Harper government is spending much less than what has been funded in its yearly budgets. This reinforces his dubious views about celebrating our differences in the name of multiculturalism, of supporting diversity rather than inclusion.

In a 2005 study by Allan Gregg's Strategic Counsel, fully 69 percent of Canadians said that immigrants should integrate and become a part of Canadian culture rather than attempt to maintain their own identity.[5] "Hyphenated" citizenship and multiculturalism is being questioned and scrutinized. Is it a positive thing to be an Italian-Canadian, an Indo-Canadian, an Irish-Canadian, a Chinese-Canadian, etcetera ad infinitum?

Economic or political support for maintaining enclaves of difference in the name of "diversity" or multiculturalism or some kind of veil of blindness is anathema to the Canadian concept. Celebration of our differences, rather than what we share in common as human beings and as human rights holders, can create long lasting resentments among Canadians. Canadians, for the most part, are a broad-minded lot and embrace such "good" words as diversity, tolerance and multiculturalism. What needs to be investigated is if limits to such notions may be appropriate as this country stumbles forward.

2. Human Rights and Multiculturalism

Multiculturalism can be defined as the "recognition and accommodation of diversity."[6] Charles Taylor has added a dimension to the concept, arguing that multiculturalism is about "due recognition…

as a vital human need."[7] These are two diametrically distinct notions worthy of analysis. Both notions focus on values, but it is important to note that multiculturalism is very much an empirical reality of North American living, let alone Canadian society.

The United States is perhaps the ultimate example of multiculturalism at work. Moynihan's sociological and Political Science classic, "The Melting Pot," was more a statement of ideological values than the real America of cultural, economic and social differences.[8] The melting pot idea is that individuals and cultural ethnicities, over time, will all blend in together and integrate seamlessly. This has not happened.

As one drives South on the I-5 freeway from Northern California to Southern California, the strong influence of the Spanish speaking Mexican diaspora on radio stations is evident. Anecdotally, it seems that almost half of such stations are delivered in Spanish by the time one reaches the Los Angeles/San Diego greater region. Many television stations are also in Spanish. This is a statement of fact, not values or what values should be implemented in a society. Multiculturalism is a continuing fact in the United States and a source of stress and schism.

Enclaves of settlement in the United States still persist. The Irish in Boston, the German influences in Minnesota and Wisconsin, the French Canadian Cajun influence in New Orleans and the Italian presence in San Francisco in such areas as North Beach are a mere sampling of the power of cultural identity. This persistence may be even greater in Canada.

Consider Little Italy in Toronto, the second largest Italian community outside of Italy itself. Check out Vancouver: Richmond is dominated by the Chinese or North Vancouver where a significant Iranian grouping calls home. The Sikh influence in the Fraser Valley in British Columbia is obvious. The English in Mount Royal in Montreal continue to thrive. The Ukrainian influence in Edmonton is lasting and they even have their own cultural village north of the city. These are realities. There has been no melting pot in either the US or Canada.

What is the link between multiculturalism and human rights? According to Jack Donnelly, human rights are "The rights one has because one is human."[9] Such rights would imply obligations upon everyone else to recognize them. In an ideal world, as Donnelly notes, such rights talk would be unnecessary.[10] All of these rights are recognized in the Canadian Charter of Rights and Freedoms, 1982, and the U.N. First order rights, as outlined in the International Covenant on Civil and Political Rights, include basic liberty rights: freedom of speech, religion, association voting rights, and so on. These have sometimes been defined as negative rights.[11] What this means is that the state has no authority to interfere in the rights of individuals to exercise these rights. Most nation-states have signed onto this Covenant.

Second order rights have been defined as positive. These are defined in the International Covenant on Economic, Social and Cultural Rights.Such rights embrace economic subsistence, health care, education, work, and housing. They are positive in the sense that states should provide them to all. The idea behind second order rights is that it is useless to have basic liberty without a full belly. This notion is much more controversial than the long tradition of liberalism and embraces Marxist ideas including the possibility of major redistribution of the fruits of economic activity to provide health care, education, social services etc. to all. Needless to say, second order rights have not secured the same United Nations support and status as first order rights. Issues of distributing the goods of a society have always taken second place to issues related to basic freedoms.

In his seminal work, A Theory of Justice, John Rawls blends these two sets of rights into a cogent and coherent iteration of where the US or any other liberal democracy should be headed.[12] He asks us to imagine an "original position" where we do not know whether we, as individuals, are wealthy or poor, and have no rights or plenty of them. We are all under an umbrella called the "veil of ignorance". He sets out two principles which are equally applicable to international politics as they are to a domestic setting.[13] The first principle is the "Liberty Principle". It states that everyone is entitled to a basic set of rights including the right to association, religion, voting rights etc. These are negative rights as noted above. No government can take them away. By extension, inter alia, such rights may include the right to education and health care and basic social services. Even though such rights may be considered to be second order rights within the U.N. declarations, they are clearly first order rights in Canada, even if they are not specifically mentioned in the Constitution Act, 1982.

Rawls's second principle, The Difference Principle, states that differences in wealth between the rich and everyone else can only be justified if they work to the advantage of the least advantaged in society. This is a quasi-Marxian notion and is not widely accepted at this point in any Western democracy, but is certainly extensively debated within academia. The second principle is not relevant to the multiculturalism discussion, but is clearly central to international discussions on human rights.

Rawls is a contractarian theorist. The key assumptions in his presentation are that anyone placed under the "veil" would accept a maximin strategy whereby they would want to maximize the minimum situation that would be their lot in society. This is based on an interpretation of rational choice. With little information provided, except knowing that the universe out there contains rich and poor people and situations where some can exercise their basic rights fully and others cannot, people will choose the same basic rights and a minimum amount of wealth. This is a limited risk strategy.

There have been strong admirers as well as detractors from the Rawls contract theory.[14] After all, there are plenty of people that would be prepared to roll the dice and hope for all rights as well as wealth. One can always hope to be a Gates or Gretzky or a Bronfmann or a Buffet, even as unlikely as those outcomes might be. Contracts are often complex. Why would anyone agree to very partial information in signing on to something that is often undecipherable? That is why people hire lawyers to interpret the meaning of a contract. Nonetheless, the original position and the veil of ignorance may be quite useful as a heuristic device to investigate and teach the meaning of fairness.

To give another example: is the following reasonable? Place a bag over a woman's head and expect her to pick the least worst possibility for a life partner, not knowing if he is nice or mean, wealthy or destitute, healthy or very ill, good looking are just plain ugly. Will she really choose average or less? Rational choice theory would say that she should choose the mundane and not gamble for better. However, why not go for bust and bet on a George Clooney or a Barack Obama? There is a certain glamour to lotto 649, even if the odds are 14 million to 1.

What is the relevance of Rawls to multiculturalism and the Canadian context? Immigrants to Canada come here under no veil of ignorance. They know that they are welcomed to this land with a long list of freedoms and rights. They are also aware of the awesome possibilities for economic work and entrepreneurial chances in which to raise their families. Unfortunately, the abject philosophy of multiculturalism allows new immigrants to group together and isolate themselves from the greater commonwealth of Canadian society.

All of the above noted rights are recognized within Canadian society. No rights are more important in this country than health care and education. In fact, surveys have shown that Canadians identify themselves principally because of their health care system. No other country in the world has defined its existence through its health care system. As previously noted, Tommy Douglas, the original founder of health care in Saskatchewan, is identified more than anyone else as the major positive historical figure in Canada for this reason.

3. Multiculturalism: Fact and Value

Multiculturalism is a bifurcated concept: fact and value. The factual part is evident everywhere in North America as previously shown. Different ethnic groups are significantly living in isolation from major populations and Canada is no exception. The questions are these: should the concept of multiculturalism be embraced as a pervasive, unending value in Canada? If so, should successive Canadian Governments be committed to support visible minorities economically indefinitely so that they can celebrate their differences with the rest of Canadians? At what price politically, economically, socially, etc. should Canadian society pay to embrace diversity or some misguided notion of group rights over inclusiveness? And how is it even possible to conceive of these two concepts as compatible?

It is a mistaken idea that multiculturalism should be embraced as a permanent value in Canada. As noted at the outset of this chapter, it is divisive and entrenches enclaves of separateness within Canada. A Canada of inclusiveness cannot be based on permanent separate quarters of living spaces in our cities, suburbs, countryside, and even educational institutions. That is a Canada of difference and it breeds fear, ignorance, intolerance, and violence. Separate enclaves are not inclusion, anymore than pervasive gated communities of the better off, principally Caucasians, throughout the land are an appropriate existence, or an entitlement to a right of exclusion. There is a certain irony to multicultural exclusivity: The isolation implodes on itself. When different cultural groups immigrate they bring their heritage, values, and distinctive quirks with them. These may have nothing to do with religious beliefs at all. This is not about dress ethnicity such as burqas or turbans or the kippah. It is about bringing over the worst parts of cultural inheritance. Honour killings within the Indo-Canadian population are absolutely unacceptable. Transporting such cultural concepts of acceptability creates animus within the greater Canadian society. It is simply unimaginable and contemptible that specific male dominated minority groups within India, Pakistan, and Afghanistan (as examples) can do whatever they want with their women after immigrating to Canada.

The most recent blatant example in Canada took place at York University in Toronto. A student from another land claimed, on religious grounds, that he should not be required to engage in group work with women to complete course assignments. York University, as noted by the professor, is composed of about 70% women and that it would be ridiculous to accommodate the request. The entire Sociology Department agreed, but the Dean of Liberal Arts of the University did not and said that the student had such a right based on religious preference. What we have here is the importation of misogynistic values, veiled as religious ones, trumping the very Charter of Rights and Freedoms relative to the equality of women. What kind of political correctness were the Dean and upper administrative echelons thinking in making such a decision? Is the intake of huge foreign tuition a consideration? Fortunately, the student backed off on the request in the end.

While the legal process and the courts address the extremes of minority group behaviour, they are unable to address patriarchal violence: what really goes on in the cocoons of private houses and apartments that is never reported? This is not to say that verbal and physical abuse does not occur in the prevailing Canadian culture. Rather, the point is that multiculturalism can be a breeding ground for the worst behaviour from other cultures. It can be interpreted by those that immigrate that they can get a free pass to continue behaviours which are increasingly not even acceptable in their own countries, as we are seeing in India and Pakistan, for example.

How far should Canadian tolerance be extended to accommodate immigrants into the Canadian fold? Should we really be prepared to allow a turban as a substitute for regular headgear in the RCMP? This absolutely undermines a country-wide symbol of oneness. Should we allow Sikh children to carry symbolic swords to school? This creates possibilities for violence. Should minorities be allowed to wear their myriad of headdresses instead of helmets on motorcycles? This defies any logic of safety and can obviously increase costs within the health care system. Canadians should be intolerant of tolerance when it breaches reasonability. Tolerance, then, has its limits, and should in any society that hopes to move forward in some semblance of harmony.

Diverse cultural peoples living in the same community in harmony never comes easily. There are suspicions and fears. For example, Robert Putnam, who studied 40 different American communities, says that a racially diverse community causes distrust and causes us to "hunker down".[15]

But these same separate racially identifiable peoples, no matter what race, are rooting within their communities and provinces for the Vancouver Canucks or the Toronto Raptors or the Edmonton Eskimos. Sports are a great leveller of income, discrimination, and everything else. And this is a good thing. They are going to the same major concerts at Rogers Arena in Vancouver. This is not multiculturalism, it is inclusion in a common identity: entertainment interests in common. This is not strength in ethnic diversity; it is power in Canadian commonality.

And yet the concept of multiculturalism holds strong within certain areas of Canada, even if it is toxic. Multiculturalism is dysfunctional to the Canadian state and should not be embraced. It is of no value to the Canadian brand and contributes to divisiveness. Group rights do not exist in U.N. declarations and neither should they be within this country. Ipso facto "group rights" recognize such misguided concepts such as multiculturalism as a value to be recognized and supported. This is a mistake. What does multiculturalism embrace?

In a hierarchy of values, diversity is not to be elevated over inclusion and integration within the greater society. Diversity breeds indifference or worse: animus toward others. The "we" of our group type trumps everything else. This leads to the isolation of different ethnic groups. It becomes a jigsaw puzzle or mosaic of different colours belonging here and there. And what is the result? The result is always the same: holding onto cultural symbols and activities in isolation. And this leads to gangs based on identity and a group identity virtually in no contact with the rest of the population. Establishing separate schools based on ethnicity cannot be positive for a future of Canada. Such schools should certainly not be bankrolled by taxpayers. Quebec seems to be aware of these problems in its nascent development of a Charter of Rights there.

4. The Quebec Charter of Values

Quebec's previous PQ Premier, Pauline Marois, proposed what some might consider a radical change in human rights within the province. Among other stipulations, government employees would no longer be allowed to wear burqas, kippahs, turbans, etcetera during their work hours.[16] The putative reasoning behind the new policy would be that citizens should not be subjected to displays of religion or specific cultural identity in the public service or in publicly supported businesses. There is every indication that the new Liberal Premier, Phillipe Couillard, will adopt and implement a similar Charter. And Quebecers as a whole are definitely onside with the Charter concept.

Allowing such headdresses and other symbols of religious identity, such as the crosses, to be paraded in schools and in other civil service venues, undermines separation of church and state and actually portrays the state as an advocate of difference and potential divisiveness. Religious, cultural symbols could certainly be portrayed as a statement; a lack of neutrality. Imagine a teenage Muslim girl that does not want to wear a veil even though her family is pushing cultural and religious background history on her. She goes to her school counselor to seek advice. The counsellor is wearing a niqab. "Allowing the social worker to wear the veil harms the teenager by preventing her from availing herself of a government service."[17]

A key French term is "laicite." Essentially, it means separation of church and state. This concept is broadly recognized in liberal democracies, although it does often go unrecognized that the US: to this day, coinages bear the motto "In God we Trust". And all children in America pledge allegiance to the country "under god" every day before school begins. So the country most identified with separation of church and state has no real separation at all! This, of course, has lead to all kinds of constitutional challenges.

"Laicite" promotes the concept of government neutrality in all things religious. Quebec's putative Charter of Values incorporates this interpretation in matters pertaining directly to government and its employees. It attempts to offer a balance between the much more intrusive and severe legislative acts in France with the Canadian Charter of Rights and Freedoms. This is a much more tolerant version reflecting the Quebec national identity. The French version banishes religious symbols completely (headdresses etcetera) in all public places.

Two different ideological perspectives seem to be in play: The Locke tradition in England and the Rousseau perspective in France. The Lockian philosophy is a philosophy of individualism which emphasizes individual rights, including a wide swath of religious rights. Tolerance is interpreted as broadly as possible. In fact, Locke wrote an essay on Tolerance (A Letter Concerning Toleration).[18.] The Rousseau perspective is grounded in the merits of a social contract. Whatever the majority agrees to in a "general will" becomes the gospel.[19] It is not nearly as amenable to individuality as Locke. But neither perspective would recognize or understand multicultural group rights. The closest recognition, but far different, would be religious tolerance.

These two ideological perspectives can partly explain the differences between English and French values. The English would be more individualistic and the French more community oriented. However, this is a simplification. The English tradition also produced perhaps its greatest philosopher, Thomas Hobbes, who very well understood the concept of contract.[20] In Leviathan (1651), he blends individualism with the necessity for security, into a fabulous logical conclusion: The state (King) is to protect the English from all foreign enemies and in exchange the citizens are to obey the will of the government. Otherwise, life would be solitary, nasty, poor, brutish and short, like his fathomed and imaginary state of nature.[21]

The proposed Quebec Charter attempts to balance individual rights with the encompassing rights of the Quebec people as a whole. It combines both the Locke interpretation of individual rights and tolerance, with the Rousseau version of a social oneness of community. Whether it has the appropriate balance will only be known through time. It is clearly much broader in terms of tolerance than the Draconian enactments in France.

Will Quebec's Charter of Values meet the constitutionality test? The short and only answer is yes. Even if the Supreme Court of Canada were to find elements of the Charter as a violation of religious or nebulous other rights, the Quebec Government would in advance, as part of its legislative procedures, make the Act subject to the Notwithstanding Clause. This is S.33 of the Charter of Rights and Freedoms, and states that a province or the federal government can opt out of s.2 and s.7-15 for a period of five years. Section 2 is the operative clause in this situation. That section includes such matters as freedom of religion and association and expression. It is also relevant to note that Quebec never signed on to the Constitution Act, 1982, and though legally subject to it constitutionally, it may be politically irrelevant to the peoples of Quebec. Passing the Charter of Rights and Freedoms and other major changes such as the amending formula without the support of one of the two founding nations within Canada will always be a source of disharmony and conflict within the federation.

5. Conclusions

Enclaves of difference within the Canadian society are contributing to the overall dysfunction of this nation-state. That such multicultural differences are actually rewarded and receive the financial support of both federal and provincial governments is abysmal. "Feel good" support is not helpful for a future of Canada and is dysfunctional since there is no real incentive, except pure economics, for minorities to blend into the Canadian mix.

Social inclusion requires governments to support a hospitable environment for inclusion and integration, including access to language services and job services. The key is to provide mechanisms for immigrants to pursue their idea of an ideal life plan within the Canadian milieu.

Celebration of our differences, rather than what binds us together as human beings, is unmitigated folly. Our human rights are as individual entitlements; in an ideal society we would not need to fight for them. Any attempts to claim "group rights" as some kind of extension of human rights is a road that leads to dead ends. It always results in divisiveness and separation, not inclusion. Iraqi ethnic conflict is a classic example of continuing strife among the Shiite, Sunni, and Kurds.

Embracing multiculturalism as a permanent value allows new immigrants to group together in isolation from the greater Canadian society of possibilities. This is clearly one of the more blatant examples of dysfunction and conflict within the Canadian union. A lack of political identity and a misdirected emphasis on multiculturalism are causes of cacophony within the Canadian federation.

Chapter 4
The Federal Spending Power

The federal spending power may be defined in this way: the unfettered capacity of the federal government to spend revenues directly and targeted to individuals, institutions, and other orders of government for some purposes outside of its jurisdictional competence to legislate. Simply put, this all-encompassing power allows Ottawa to fund programs for which it may not be able to legislate or regulate directly. With or without provincial consent, the spending power has been used as a kind of Trojan horse to intrude into jurisdictions for which it has no responsibility. The consequences for the Canadian federation have been enormous and, once again, illustrate the dysfunctional nature of the political system.

This chapter addresses the constitutional basis of the spending power, the federal and provincial arguments, and its overall dysfunctional results for the federation. It is about federal revenues taken in and where or where not they should be spent.

Constitutional Basis

Constitutionally, there are a number of sources in the Constitution Act, 1867, which have been interpreted to provide the federal government with the authority to spend outside of its jurisdictional competence. These include: s.91 (1A), the power to regulate with respect to public debt and property; s.93, the raising of revenue by any mode or system of taxation; s.106, the power to appropriate public funds. Additional sources could include s.102, creating the Consolidated Revenue Fund, and, perhaps s.91(4), allowing Ottawa to borrow money. S.36 (1 and 2) in the Constitution Act, 1982, addresses regional disparities and equalization. The latter commits Parliament "...to provide reasonably comparable levels of public services at reasonably comparable levels of taxation." No doubt, the preamble to s.91, the residual Peace, Order and Good Government clause, augments the other constitutional sources of federal powers to spend.

It was not always so easy for the federal government to spend directly and intrude in areas of specific provincial jurisdiction. The Judicial Committee of the Privy Council in the U.K. ruled in a seminal constitutional case that even though Parliament may raise revenue by any means of taxation, it does not follow that it can dispose of such revenue by any means. The Court said: "It still may be legislation affecting the classes of subjects in s.92, and, if so, would be ultra vires."[1] By spending, the federal government can unconstitutionally encroach upon provincial fields of jurisdiction.

This has been specifically referred to as the "watertight compartments" conception of federalism where each government should only tend to, and spend in, its own fields of exclusive jurisdiction as outlined in sections 91 and 92 of the Constitution Act, 1867. The problem with the watertight conception is that constitutional and fiscal federalism does not readily lend itself to the analogy of a great big shipping vessel where shutting off areas and sealing them tight could save and keep it afloat. Such technological engineering could not even save the Titanic!

The Canadian depression in the 1930's clearly provided an impetus for greater federal involvement in providing substantive programs to individuals to address unemployment and welfare issues. The Royal Commission on Dominion-Provincial Relations (Rowell-Sirois Commission) was authorized in 1937 to assess the distribution of legislative powers, the economic basis of confederation and economic disparities within the nation.[2] One of its key recommendations was that unemployment insurance should be addressed directly through federal legislation. It should be noted that it had been determined by the Supreme Court and then the Judicial Committee of the Privy Council in the previously noted reference case in 1937 that unemployment insurance fell under provincial jurisdiction: property and civil rights (s.92(13)). Therefore, it was outside of federal competence.

Nonetheless, all provinces ceded jurisdiction in 1940 so that unemployment insurance could be provided nationally by the federal government. It was a major admission on the part of provincial jurisdictions that they did not have the fiscal wherewithal to fund such a program adequately. There was also the recognition that citizens' mobility from province to province could be furthered through a national program. This was a major concession: the first significant delegation of power from one order of government to the other.

Provinces no longer have control over this area and the citizens of some provinces have been very unfairly impacted by changes which treat workers differently in different provinces. Severe discriminatory practices have been injected into the program that could never have happened had provincial agreement been required to make significant changes, as is the case with the Canada Pension Plan, an area of joint federal-provincial jurisdiction.

The federal government is using its federal spending power to distort mobility and to favour some regions over others. And changing the formula from a weeks-worked based system to an hours-worked one has resulted in a huge decrease in the numbers eligible to receive employment insurance: from 70% to around 40%. As noted by Eugenie Brouillet, federal efficiencies are taking precedence over diversity.[3] The Employment Insurance Act Reference case (1975) further augmented federal power by extending maternity and parental benefits. Such extension undermines the Property and Civil Rights clause in s.92(13), thereby extending the scope of federal power over social matters that the provinces had specifically refused to transfer to the federal Parliament in 1940.[4]

EI contributions have basically become a slush fund for the federal government to use as it sees fit. That monies go directly from employees into the Federal consolidated Revenue Fund is telling. As administered, the unemployment system has obviously added to the dysfunctional nature of the Canadian political system. There could be no better an example of "tax and spend" at will and in accordance with federal priorities, even if these cause injustices, distortions, inefficiencies, and mobility issues. It is of little consequence to those being denied benefits that a significant amount of these funds may be going to decrease the size of the yearly deficit.

In 1941, the Tax Rental Agreements were agreed to in all jurisdictions. World War II was certainly the major, but not the only, reason for the provinces to cede tax room to the federal government so that sufficient revenues could be raised to fight the war. Certainly, there was also an imbalance between the revenue raising capacity of poorer provinces relative to wealthier ones and this was also a raison d'être for a severely altered conception of federalism.

"Simply stated, the Tax Rental Agreements were a system by which the provincial governments accept to "rent", to give up to the federal government the three standard direct taxes (personal and corporate taxes and succession duties) for a limited period of time, in return for payment to each province of certain fixed sums of money."[5] This augmented the federal spending power in ways not imaginable at the time. The war clearly undermined the autonomy and powers of the provinces.

In 1962, the Federal-Provincial Fiscal Arrangements Act provided for the federal government to collect provincial taxes as well as their own. In exchange, provinces, except Quebec, agreed to acknowledge the federally determined tax base (what is taxed) and tax as a percentage of that base. Alberta and Ontario would collect their own corporate taxes separately from personal income tax. While provinces have strayed a bit with various deductions and credits, as assented to by Federal Finance, the basic structure is the same today: provincial tax is a percentage of federal tax. In exchange for this "national" form of taxation, the federal government lowered its tax rates and most provinces filled the vacated tax room.

It was not until the advent of Established Programs Financing (1977), block-funding for health care and education, that the provinces successively clawed back a greater portion of the tax room lost during the war. Block funding (no conditions) replaced Shared Cost Financing (50-50 cost-shared, dependent on provincial spending triggering federal spending). The Canada Health Act (1985) placed conditions on the transfer. Fiscal transfers will be discussed in depth in a later chapter. A key point is that the federal government never readily relinquishes powers it has secured. There may be an iron rule of politics and economy at work here: More sources of tax revenues means more ways in which the government in possession of those revenues can supply benefits to its citizens; tax and spend may causally lead to winning elections. Powers of taxation are a magical, powerful elixir for which there may be no substitutes in the political world. Charismatic personalities may move sentiment, but taxes can provide income support.

The federal principle is the ultimate bulwark against implementation of the federal spending power. This principle delineates the powers in s.91 and s.92 and the shared fields. It means this: these are the key split areas which the Founders divided between the federal government and the provinces and they are to be respected. As stated by Brouillet, "The distribution of legislative powers constitutes the very heart of the federal principle."[6] Even though the watertight conception is no longer relevant, given duplication, overlapping, and the sheer lack of provincial/territorial revenues between the two jurisdictions, elusive attempts at cooperative federalism have seldom been successful.

Court Cases

Court decisions have certainly extended the federal spending function since the Constitution Act, 1982. No doubt, enshrining the Charter of Rights and Freedoms into that document has emboldened the Court in other matters as well, including the interpretation of the breadth and extent of the federal spending power. Inclusion of s.36(1) into the Act (Equalization and Regional Disparities) putatively adds a dimension to the spending power which was absent before. This section actually specifies a rationale for the use of the spending power in the provinces which was non-existent: an ephemeral act of Parliament is now a powerful, permanent constitutional provision. Future court decisions could very well cite this provision to extend the meaning of the spending power in the future.

A number of contemporary Court decisions are significant. The first is Finlay v. Canada {1986}, which upholds federal conditions contained in the Canada Assistance Plan (CAP).[7] A second is Reference re: Canada Assistance Plan (BC), 1991.[8] The program provided 50/50 cost-shared funding for welfare (payments to recipients and operating expenditures) in the provinces. The federal government unilaterally limited funding increases to 5% yearly, in order to cap its expenditures, particularly to the wealthier provinces of Ontario, British Columbia and Alberta. The essential question was whether the federal government could do so constitutionally, since these were bi-lateral agreements with each province and provided for open-ended funding. The Court reaffirmed the Parliamentary Sovereignty doctrine which "prevents a legislative body from binding itself as to the substance of future legislation"[9]. Justice Sopinka went further: "The Court should not, under the overriding principle of federalism, supervise the federal government's exercise of its spending power in order to protect the autonomy of the provinces".[10] There was "no colourable attempt to regulate in provincial areas of jurisdiction", therefore no limitation on federal powers.[11]

Clearly, the Court was not willing to consider the inherent value of bi-lateral and federal-provincial agreements in the balance, and resorted to Parliamentary Supremacy as the overarching consideration. And since there was no arguable attempt to regulate directly in an area of provincial jurisdiction, there was no spending power issue. What the Court refused to address was that the federal government entered into these agreements under one set of premises and then reneged, thereby straining provincial revenue funds and undoing legitimate expectations. Such unilateral federal decisions cause fractures and bad will in this federation.

The Court seems to want to be steadfast in holding to a narrow interpretation of the spending power: Is there an attempt to regulate in an area of provincial jurisdiction? Reducing federal contributions certainly impacts provincial programs, severely in some cases, forcing provinces to re-regulate their own programs: in this case, potentially lowering benefits. That such federal financial decisions obviously have a significant impact on provincial finances is of no account.

A third case is Winterhaven Stables Ltd. V. Canada (1988)[12]. In this case, the constitutionality of the Income Tax Act was questioned, saying that is was ultra vires Parliament because portions of such payments were transferred to fund provincial programs.[13] At the Court of Appeal level in Alberta, the conclusions were as follows: 1, the legislation was not in relation to provincial legislation over health, education, and welfare, but only financial assistance; 2, Parliament is entitled to spend through the "proper" use of its taxing power; 3, Parliament can impose conditions as long as there is not an attempt to control or regulate; 4, In some cost-shared programs there is an opting out provision.[14] An appeal to the Supreme Court was denied.

This is the closest enunciation of a "reading in" doctrine to the Constitution Acts, 1867 and 1982, so far in respect to the spending power. It is important to note that there is no specific heading of power or reference to such a power in the Constitution. However, it seems that the "breathing tree" interpretation of the Constitution is at work here: "The BNA Act planted in Canada a living tree capable of expansion..." (1929).[15] What this means is that the Constitution should be interpreted in a flexible manner, rather than rigidly. And since 1982, the Canadian courts have not been shy in perceiving constitutional documents as malleable and supple.

It is one thing to extend Charter of Rights and Freedoms matters to include, for example, same sex marriage (Reference re: Same sex marriage(2004).[16] But it is a stretch to stray from Canadian citizens' rights as enunciated in the Charter of Rights and Freedoms into the entire field of spending in federal- provincial fiscal agreements. Such spill-over notions definitely undermine the spirit of cooperative federalism. Much of the European Union experiment has been predicated on patterned fancies of spill-over: that one cooperative area would spill-over into others, from the economic to the political, eventually engulfing them all into some form of harmonious union. Ernest Haas coined the spill-over notion.[17] The results have been very mixed.

The 1998 Quebec reference case reaffirms the federal principle: that federalism is a fundamental characteristic of Canada, along with the rule of law, democracy and respect for minorities: Federalism "recognizes the diversity of the component parts of Confederation, and the autonomy of provincial governments to develop their societies within their spheres of jurisdiction."[18] As Telford contends, a future spending power court case could hinge on whether overarching principles of federalism supersede an unlimited power of the federal government to spend in areas outside their jurisdiction.[19]

Governments do not give up autonomous powers readily, and the hypothetical, ethereal spending power in Canada can certainly be implemented in ways which undermine provincial/territorial powers. While the Courts cannot be expected to 'take leave' of the spending power debates in the future, it should behoove them to tread carefully as national citizens' rights and freedoms are quite distinct and separate from corporal bodies like provinces. Provinces are constitutionally and solely responsible for providing healthcare, education at all levels, welfare, and a myriad of other services to *their* citizens. It may be an unintended accident or effect of Canadian constitutional history, but the *most* important activities and services that all governments world-wide are engaged in, except such matters as defense and printing currency, devolve to the provinces in Canada, so realities must be addressed.

The Federal Perspective on the Spending Power

Perhaps the federal government's definition of the spending power was best articulated in 1969 and there has been no budging from this position since. Trudeau stated: It is "the power of Parliament to make payments to people or institutions or governments for purposes on which it (Parliament) does not have the power to legislate."[20] Peter Hogg has certainly given academic support for this position. "The issue is whether the spending power authorizes payments for objects which are outside federal legislative competence."[21]

His answer: "Parliament may spend or lend its funds to any government or institution or individual it chooses, for any purpose it chooses. And may attach any conditions it chooses. There is a distinction between compulsory regulation and spending involving obligations voluntarily assumed by the recipient."[22] According to this perspective, a willing provincial recipient of federal spending such as a cost-shared or block-funded program must assume the consequences of such agreement, even if the result is *regulation* of an exclusive area of provincial jurisdiction. Yet any attempt at regulation is specifically forbidden as per the above noted Labour Conventions case, 1937. Moreover, to claim willy-nilly that such obligations are voluntarily assumed represents a basic misunderstanding of the dynamics of federal-provincial meetings, negotiations, and obligations of provinces to their citizens. When provinces lack the fiscal capacity to carry out their constitutional responsibilities, they usually accept monies to help do so, even if submitting to unconstitutional conditions are included. There is no voluntariness operating here; provincial room to manoeuvre is severely constricted. This is a kind of forced federalism, which is in itself an oxymoron. This is particularly pertinent during economic downturns when provincial revenues suffer declines of personal, corporate, and other taxes, even when demands for the basic social programs (health, education, welfare) continue to increase.

A refusal to accept funds is a non-starter in all provinces, except maybe Quebec and Alberta. Quebec's reasons would always be based almost exclusively on jurisdictional issues. Alberta's rejection would be a bit more nuanced, based on both constitutional reasons as well as sheer fiscal means. There is only one taxpayer, and taxpayers do not understand when governments cannot come to mutual agreement to secure funds for programs. Verrelli makes a similar point: "It is questionable to assert that the provinces have a choice to accept or refuse the federal funds; they cannot in good conscience deny their citizens social programs by refusing to accept or refuse money, at least some of which has been collected by the federal government."[23]

The spending power took on particular importance in the aftermath of Rene Levesque's and Quebec's decision not to assent to the changes included in the patriation of the Constitution Act, 1982. Whether *any* government committed to secession could have agreed to the changes is a matter of continuing conjecture in both government and academic circles. One of the incessant, persistent problems of contemporary federalism is that Quebec is not a signatory to the Act. In an important sense, Quebecers are disenfranchised, and successive provincial governments and Quebecers are well aware of that.

Certainly, the more amenable, compromising Bourassa Government in Quebec thought it was worthwhile in 1985 to pursue five conditions as a means to "re-enfranchise" their citizens. And the spending power was one of them. Many teleconference and "mano a mano" meetings transpired. The product was the Meech Lake Accord, to which all governments agreed in 1987. The spending power provision says, "The Government of Canada shall provide reasonable compensation to the government of a province that chooses not to participate in a national shared-cost program that is established by the Government of Canada after the coming into force of this section in an area of exclusive provincial jurisdiction, if the province carries on a program or initiative that is compatible with the national objectives." The federal government, under Prime Minister Mulroney, wholeheartedly endorsed this spending power condition as well as the other provisions of the Accord. The Accord ultimately failed, as both Newfoundland and Manitoba did not ratify it in their legislatures. "Executive federalism," decision-making by First Ministers and intergovernmental elites, seemed to be on a precipice, an inter-governance cliff.

The Meech Lake Accord spending power provision was replicated in the Charlottetown Accord (1992): A province could opt out of a "national shared-cost program" and receive compensation as long as it carried out a program compatible with national objectives. From a federal view, the federal spending power would be enshrined in the Constitution, even if its stretch would be nebulous. Provinces opting out of a national program would be required to develop comparable programs in order to receive their fair share of funding. Entrenching the federal spending power without *ever* explicitly referencing it would have been a clear coup for the federal government, and would have given Courts an extra aspect to lean on in making future decisions.

The Charlottetown Accord was ultimately put to the test of the people and it was turned down in six provinces. Even 'nationalist' oriented Ontario barely accepted it, and it was rejected in all of the Western provinces. It was the consummate rejection by the Canadian people of government elites attempting to direct this shaky ship of state. Canadians were confused about its contents and slighted by the lack of understandable information available to them about its meaning. So-called appended "consensus documents" to consider this and that in the future augmented the atmosphere of unknowing. Who would vote for a comprehensive document that would require a PhD in Political Science and Constitutional Law to comprehend? What the elite could no longer get directly on their own through executive federalism or federal and provincial legislatures, they tried to get indirectly through an obfuscated national referendum. How upside down could a process be in a Parliamentary system? Edmund Burke, a well-known MP in England, would not have approved, as his perspective was that once elected, MPs should make their own decisions as representatives, rather than poll citizens ad nauseum.

Ironically, many of the direct participants in the process that actually put pen to paper in good faith to write it probably voted against the Accord for a myriad of reasons. The spending power provision was certainly one of them. The entire process was a "dog's breakfast," as some participants have said, but as well it was an honest attempt at attempting to bring Quebec into the constitutional fold once and for all. It was also an appeal to First Nations' Peoples, women, and minorities. The accommodative Canadian attempt to land on shore failed on the shoals of a very rocky, dysfunctional federal system.

Parizeau's separatist Pequiste Quebecois government consequently called for the October 1995 Referendum, establishing some kind of nebulous independent Quebec based on sovereignty association (similar to the 1982 Referendum). The Referendum result was close to 50-50, and it lost by a threadbare .6% (six tenths of one percent or about 54,000 votes out of 4.7 million cast. Prime Minister Chretien and Intergovernmental Affairs Minister Dion were clearly shaken by the result. The Secession Reference Case (1998) and the Clarity Act (2000), specifying the conditions under which a province could separate, were the products of the Referendum.

In September 1996, Dion articulated and hinted at his support for this view: "Some Canadian constitutional experts believe that the federal spending power has been recognized by the courts as a means for the Government of Canada to fulfil its constitutional responsibility to maintain peace, order and good government."[24] Extending the spending power's connotation in this way would give this hypothetical, unwritten, non-constitutionalized power the same status as the real *constitutional*, overarching Peace, Order and Good Government clause. The "read-in" spending power could become a kind of supernova power within s.91 that could override all other provincial powers included in s.92 and s.93 etc.

The Harper government promised to usher in a new era of harmonious federal provincial relations. In good faith, it started with Quebec: It legislated that Quebec is a nation within a united Canada. On the spending power, it stated in the October 2007 Throne Speech that they would be "…guided by our principle of openness, our Government will introduce legislation to place formal limits on the use of the federal spending power for new cost shared programs in areas of exclusive provincial jurisdiction. This legislation will allow provinces and territories to opt out with reasonable compensation if they offer compatible programs."[25] As of 2014, no such legislation has been passed. And Harper will not even meet with Premiers to discuss the future financing of health care, post-secondary education, or welfare, surely a sign of trepidation or just plain defiance. He is in perpetual trepidation of them!

From the Victoria Charter (1971) to Meech Lake (1985) to the Charlottetown Accord (1992) to the present, there has been no unanimous agreement on the meaning, extent, or even de jure existence of the spending power. Nevertheless, the federal government continues to spend copiously outside its jurisdictional competence. And the de facto spending power is an important and necessary reality of the current state of federal- provincial existence, given the overall lack of financial capacity in the provinces.

What are the principal arguments that can be made in favour of some kind of federal government spending power? No, doubt, the first encompassing narrative would outline the need for nation-wide programs which must be directed from a centralized national government. Uniform programs have a certain wide appeal. The idea is that Ottawa (or Washington, Beijing, Mexico City etc.) knows better what is best for the provinces or states or regions. Let the provinces and localities administer federally determined acts, regulations and rules from the centre. This has been called Administrative Federalism. In its most extreme incarnation, provinces would lose jurisdiction over the formulation of laws in their very own areas of jurisdiction. This would be an undermining and denial of the federal principle.

A second argument would be if the federal government does spend in the provinces, it should have some say in the development of the shape of national programs. This is a "pay to play" concept; the converse is: no pay, no say. This argument would speak to how much involvement in provincial jurisdiction is acceptable as the result of providing compensation. A third issue is accountability. If the federal government grants funds to provinces, taxpayers expect some accountability for the expenditure of those monies: are they producing the intended results? Are they doing so in an efficient and timely manner? Fourth, the federal government claims it should be given visibility for funds transferred, whether this be a show of shovels or other official announcements by all governments. Visibility for funds dispensed means potential re-election and, if not that, glorification for perceived deeds accomplished.

The theme throughout the use of the federal spending power, from a federal viewpoint, is that somehow Ottawa must take charge in defining citizenship and the economic obligations and rights that transpire therefrom. Somehow, citizenship is becoming a putative federal responsibility, and one of the key ways to honour that responsibility is through spending; the spending power has become a way for the federal government to take charge and to attempt to reduce provinces to administrators of the federal largesse. This has been a blatant attempt to use the Charter of Rights of Freedoms in the legal and political rights fields and spill it over into the constitutionally non-existent economic arena. The strategy has been partly successful from the late 1990s up until the present, as will be further explored in the chapter on federal-provincial relations.

Provincial Perspectives on the Spending Power

Successive federal governments have spoken fairly consistently on their position on the federal spending power, while provincial governments have different interests, capabilities, and sentiments toward federal spending in their exclusive fields of jurisdiction. "Show me the money," and its potential consequences, means something different for Quebec and, at times, Alberta, than all other jurisdictions.

The bottom line for Quebec is that any new, cost-shared programs must involve equitable compensation without conditions on funding as long as comparable programs are devised in the province. Their first preference would be equal per capita funding and no conditions at all on where the money is spent. Any which way the words are twisted or rearranged in Meech Lake or Charlottetown or various federal throne speeches etc., Quebec's position has been formidable and remarkably consistent for over fifty years. First, it seeks to entrench watertight sovereignty within its areas of jurisdiction; and second, it seeks "profitable federalism." Quebec stays in the Canadian federation poker game so long as the money poured in far exceeds what goes out.

The watertight conception is best reflected in Premier Duplessis' thinking. He contended that the "federal authority and the provincial authority are both sovereign within the limits of their attributions," as quoted by Telford.[26] He added: "The Canadian Constitution consecrates the exclusive rights of the provinces to legislate respecting matters in regards to education, hospitals, asylums, institutions and charitable homes and public works all of which touch on property and civil rights."[27]

This position has been reiterated in one way or another ever since. The Pepin Robarts Commission in 1980 argued for opting out with compensation. Premier Levesque, at the 1984 Annual Premiers Conference, summarized the Quebec position: "We have lost count of the 'national' subjects that Ottawa intends to impose by using its spending power…" and "We are seeing a mutation of what the essence of Canadian federalism has been the provinces' areas of jurisdiction are no longer even considered exclusive by Ottawa, which arrogates the right to intervene for every purpose…"[28] He went on to articulate a federal offensive that essentially assumes that provinces are ill-equipped to fulfil their own jurisdictional responsibilities.

Premier Bourassa's Intergovernmental Affairs Minister, Gil Remillard, in May 1986, said this: "At present there is no exclusive provincial jurisdiction that is not susceptible in either a direct or indirect way to being affected by the federal spending power. The spending power has become a sword of Damocles hanging menacingly over any province wanting to plan its social, cultural or economic development."[29] In 1991, the Belanger-Campeau Commission on the Political and Constitutional Future of Quebec called for: "…a division of powers and responsibilities over those matters and domains which already fall under its exclusive jurisdiction which means eliminating in these domains the federal spending power and overlapping interventions."[30]

At the Annual Premiers' Conference in August 1997, Quebec expressed this concern: "An intergovernmental mechanism to formulate national standards applicable to social programs would thus pose a direct threat to Quebecer's existing prerogative and responsibilities in defining and managing its social policy, exercised under its exclusive jurisdiction in the field."

And in December 1997, Quebec's Intergovernmental Affairs Minister Brassard contended: "…the federal government is conducting a policy it describes as administrative reform of the federation. One of the primary elements of this reform is to crystallize and legitimize the reinforcement of the role it has arrogated itself in the fields of social matters, a sector which falls under Quebec's jurisdiction." He went much further: "The provinces of English Canada are participating actively in the centralization by agreeing to recognize formally that Ottawa has a leading role in these matters."[31] Quebec's concerns always rest most importantly on jurisdictional sovereignty and eschewing any attempts to control basic legislative and policy matters. This is also a concern in several other provinces, including Alberta.

From Quebec Premiers Levesque, to Parizeau, Bourassa, and Charest, there is a consistent pattern and rallying call: provincial sovereignty is best compartmentalized into hermetic cargo containers. Ideally, this would mean that there would be absolutely no federal involvement in health, education, social services or a myriad of other programs, some of which obviously include direct transfers from the federal government to individuals through the tax system. Opting out with full compensation and no conditions would be the holy grail of federalism in Quebec. A counter perspective would be that 1, federal taxpayer money needs to be accountable to all citizens; and 2, disparate programs in each province lead to what Prime Minister Trudeau coined 'checkerboard federalism' with all of the attendant consequences of that. Dissimilar programs obviously lead to inequalities and differences among provinces.

This has sometimes been referred to as "profitable federalism." Successive Quebec governments and some business elites support continued participation in Confederation so long as the pros and cons of fiscal economics benefit them. A constricted, castrated notion of the federal spending power is essential to this view. At the same time, this plus and minus game of federalism is anathema to the thinking and basic sentiments in most other parts of Canada. What could be more counterproductive to a working federal system than an incessant "what is in it for Quebec?" Or any other province, for that matter? "Federal pay, but no right to play," is not in the cards.

Alberta's position on the spending power has been both less strident and less clear than Quebec's.[32] Alberta has been more willing to assent to new cost-shared programs as long as the province participated in the formulation of them. Economically, Alberta is also responsible to its taxpayers since they contribute an overwhelmingly disproportionate amount of taxes to the national coffers relative to any other province. So, of course, this affects the dialogue. As Premier Klein pontificated in 1999, "Ottawa is the city where our tax dollars come to die."[33]

Conversely, Alberta wants to be perceived as a cooperative player, and perhaps the most accurate way to describe its position is in Principle Seven of the Calgary Declaration (1988): "Canada is a federal system where federal, provincial and territorial governments work in partnership while respecting each other's jurisdiction." As natural resource wealth affects almost everything else in the province, the additional protections set out in s.92A of the Constitution Act, 1982, in the aftermath of the National Energy Program (1980) have assuaged much of Alberta's jurisdictional concerns. The 7-50 Amending formula (largely an Alberta creation) contained in the same Act has also given a lasting role to Alberta as a participant in the federation. A palpable envy, though, is always present in Alberta intergovernmental circles about the strength of Quebec's disentanglement positions. It is both a matter of trepidation a conundrum: How far would such positions receive acceptance within the general populace over time? Under the surface politics between the Conservative Party and Wild Rose are surely considering these matters. Who would have thought that the Conservative party in Alberta would be atrophied in this way after forty four years in power?

The preference for both Alberta and Quebec would be for tax points, additional tax room to carry out their constitutionally required responsibilities. Essentially, the federal government would tax less and the provinces would swallow up the tax room to provide new and existing programs and undertakings. Like the block-funded Established Programs Financing program of 1977 (EPF), there is a stubborn recalcitrance on the part of federal governments to pursue this course, even if it would ameliorate, in a major way, the tensions over the use and misuse of the spending power. More of this will be elucidated on the chapter on fiscal transfers.

All provinces in 2013, except Alberta, Saskatchewan, and Newfoundland are now equalization-receiving provinces. Receiving provinces' room to manoeuvre in spending areas is limited. Even debt ridden, manufacturing Ontario is looking more like California, Florida, or Michigan than any province in Canada. The consequence is a certain susceptibility to take revenues anyhow, anyway, and under any circumstances. This is particularly true of the Maritime provinces, Newfoundland, and Manitoba. They are often prepared to give in on jurisdiction as an existential economic and political reality when new programs are developed or established programs renewed, whether they be cost-shared, block-funded or direct spending to individuals. To do otherwise, in their perspectives, would be to do an irresponsible disservice to their citizens. Dangling new federal monies in front of provincial Finance Ministers is a powerful temptation and elixir for which there are few, if any, substitutes.

Conclusions

Provincial arguments against the spending power are the inverse of the federal government's arguments for it. First, there is no "spending power" clause. It is legally non-extant. The 1937 inter-delegation decision solved that once and for all. Any clever attempts to argue that the spending power is a gift or that S.94 can somehow be extended to include all provinces when it has not even been used to extend influence or inter-delegate responsibilities in Ontario, Nova Scotia, or New Brunswick is dream-weaving.[34]

Second, the fact that the spending power is a "reality," kind of like bullying in school, only establishes a political fact: pay, or no play. In this case, provinces pay with their autonomy. This political reality is discordant to any kind of permanent Canadian union as it contradicts the federal principle: the basic equality of both orders of government. Political realities are meant to be changed in political ways and not through constitutionally determined ones. The Social Union Agreement (1999) was an elusive mechanism that attempted to do just that.[35] It was destined to fail without Quebec's support or sober intergovernmental heads in command in some provinces.

Third, provinces argue that they are the best guardian of citizens' political and economic rights within their jurisdictions. Governments that are closer to their citizens are usually considered within Canada to be better guarantors of their rights and well-being. Ironically, this argument is coming under very close scrutiny in any number of US states as "states rights" often take away such rights.

Remote central governments may think in more universal and global ways but have very little relevance to day to day living experiences in each of the provinces. Ottawa and Ontario are simply not synonymous with this country. Accountability and closeness to one's citizens seems to make more sense.

Fourth, provinces lack the fiscal capacity to carry out their constitutionally mandated responsibilities. Instead of using its financial largesse to help fund the overriding responsibilities for health, education, and social services, the legitimate alternatives would be to do three things: 1, transfer additional tax room to the provinces; 2, substantially supplement the Equalization Program; and 3, augment the block-funded Canada Health Transfer and the Canada Social Transfer. An appropriate and significant tax transfer would make the latter unnecessary.

Fifth, recognition of Quebec as a distinct society (a nation within a country or more), establishes claims to language and cultural society which presumably distinguish it from other regions. This "French fact" from the onset of Confederation would be a strong argument for disentanglement along the lines suggested above. Quebec would be enabled to develop its own programs on its own terms and receive unfettered compensation in the block-funded programs, Equalization, etc. Let's be clear: the constitutional possibilities of ratification of this idea is very unlikely.

All Quebec play, but no Ottawa say! The problems with this perspective are obvious. They lead into an asymmetrical type of federation which is simply unacceptable in the provinces that disproportionately , depending on the year, bankroll the federation: Ontario, Alberta, Saskatchewan and BC Taxation, without benefit, or unequal benefit, may be as dramatic, or even more so, than the classic Boston Tea Party reality of taxation without representation. Hogg calls this taxation without benefit.[36]

It is more insidious in the sense that the citizens of those provinces are paying more than their fair share for the social programs yet see fewer transfers inflowing. Conversely, taxation without representation has a certain clarity to it. Petter's outstanding and prophetic article, *Federalism and the Myth of the Spending Power,"* put it this way: "An electorate that cannot attribute political responsibility to one order of government or the other lacks…the ability to express its political will [then] the spending power compromises political accountability."[37] Citizens then no longer know who is responsible for what. This is extremely dysfunctional for a political system based on responsible government where parliaments are supposedly responsible to their citizens. When the paying function becomes confused with the administrative function, then there is an obfuscation and blurring of who to blame for what, or who to credit for what.

Chapter 5
Institutions

1. History

Canada is a poorly built nation. Any entity based and constructed upon a weak foundation will ultimately fracture and crumble. The institutions have never reflected the political, economic, cultural and social realities of this country. What were the Charlottetown founders thinking? They agreed to a political system that would be similar to the British system: A House of Commons and an appointed Senate similar in principle to that of the United Kingdom. And S.9, Constitution Act, 1867, says that executive power is to be "vested in the Queen." (S.91) is as clear as crystal: "It shall be lawful for the Queen, with the advice and consent of the Senate and House of Commons, to make laws for the Peace, Order and Good Government of Canada." This has been referred to as the Residual Clause of the Constitution and has often been interpreted to give Ottawa wide-sweeping powers to legislate and regulate in areas not exclusively granted to the provinces.

As if to underscore federal power, the Founders designed s.92 (10c) which provides that works wholly situated within a province but are for the general advantage of Canada, when affecting two or more provinces, are within the federal domain. This is referred to as the Declaratory Power, although it may well be inoperable now except in the most extraordinary circumstances such as war.

In the preamble to the Constitution Act, 1867, it states that Canada is to have "a Constitution similar in Principle to that of the United Kingdom."

Lower and Upper Canada (Quebec and Ontario) along with New Brunswick and Nova Scotia agreed to the Union. Quebec never embraced this deal wholeheartedly. Why would they? To pay heed to a queen that is not of their making would make no sense. To agree to a parliamentary system far removed from the French Presidential system was surely anathema to their first political instincts.

Institutions implying the Supremacy of Parliament include the House of Commons, the Senate and the Queen (Governor General and Lieutenant Governors in the provinces). The system agreed to in 1867 was clearly intended to be similar to the United Kingdom. The first Prime Minister, Sir John A. Macdonald, was definitely a centralist, but clearly understood that to bring together the constituent units would require compromise including the long list of provincial powers in (s.92).

With their eyes intently fixated on the strength of the US in the aftermath of the Civil War (1861-1865), and voices across the border calling for some version of Manifest Destiny or invasion, the compromises made to bring all parties to agreement may have seemed small at the time. Outcomes of a US invasion would have been far-reaching; a repeat of any US losses of the magnitude of The War of 1812 would not have happened, given the huge military build-up in the Northern US. Canada surely would have been subsumed under the American banner.

Clearly, the Canadian Founders had their eyes fixated on the United States and not only because of the fear of invasion. The 15,000 or so Loyalists that fled the US revolution founded new homesteads in Canada, mainly in Ontario and Nova Scotia, with a smattering in Quebec and New Brunswick. They brought with them their values from New England and elsewhere. While these numbers seem miniscule by today's diaspora, they were significant enough to alter the Canadian political identity in ways no one could have imagined. Even though they were committed to a continued British presence, they were also enamoured with a distribution of powers between governments that would ultimately limit the power of the central government in Canada, and result in a federal system that has strayed far afield from a true parliamentary, unitary system of government.

Why did Quebec agree to this faulted and slipshod arrangement? Ultimately, Quebec would rather be part of a poorly conceived Canada than face the direct possibility of being invaded and controlled by the Americans. After all, the US was feeling muscular and aggressive in the aftermath of the overwhelming victory of the North over the South in the US civil war.

Ontario similarly feared an imminent American invasion. So it was better to unite than let the simmering tensions between Ontario and Quebec, dating from the Plains of Abraham in Quebec City, shape their future. Hence, Canada, from the outset, was defined mainly by externalities rather than a collective élan or esprit de corps or common soul or any idea whatsoever of an ethos. Nation-states typically require an internal raison d'être for a lasting foundation.

Of course, there were additional reasons for uniting. It was hoped that trade would substantially increase among the joining provinces, and the vision of a lucrative East-West national railway similar to the massive US railway system was a project that could only happen with Union. The business barons in Canada were pressing the politicians hard. And the promise of a railroad in Nova Scotia was sufficient to bring that province into this union, rather than join the US

This national policy would be based on tying together the East and West with the railway, and with exorbitant tariffs which would limit Canadians, but specifically the West, from buying US manufactured goods such as tractors etc. From the beginning, the Founders were intent on making Canada more than mere "hewers of wood and drawers of water." But their definition of Canada was on Upper and Lower Canada and not so much on the other parts. Population mass certainly trumped sparsely rural areas.

Moreover, Britain showed little interest in continuing with the colonization of Canada, particularly since they had supported a losing cause with the South in the American Civil War. They were not prepared to bankroll Canada any longer. The risks exceeded the benefits, in their estimation.

Perhaps nationhood can exist for generations based on external threats (but not for millennia). Germany has clearly mastered this reality in the aftermath of losing two World Wars. And surely the US has hopefully learned this lesson in that the Vietnam War, rather than uniting the people, divided Americans in ways not envisioned since the Civil War. However, the recent wars in Iraq and Afghanistan, the longest wars in American history, are not encouraging.

While initial and formative nation-building can indeed be moved forward by raising the specter of external enemies, even Machiavelli, in The Discourses, preferred a republic based on good education and good habits of the people. Internal nation-building, augmented with appropriate political institutions, would be preferred over tyranny rationalized and embellished with external threats. When the institutions of government do not match the political realities something has to give. It is impossible to have a system that is based on a British style of government coexist with a federal system based on the equality of the provincial units. It is an obvious contradiction that has not gone unnoticed.

Thomas Hobbes, in the seminal work Leviathan, clearly supported a unitary form of government where separate parts and factions would be required to pay due heed and respect to the central authority. As previously noted, the idea was that total, centrally controlled power would protect the people of the United Kingdom from anarchy where life would be "nasty, brutish and short". All of this was to rationalize total power under the auspices of a king. External threats were indeed a prominent and overarching concern, even though England did have the advantage of geographical isolation from Europe.

"Unitarism," or a unitary form of government, does not interact well with federal systems which recognize two or more orders of government. The United Kingdom's political democracy is based on the Supremacy of Parliament. Decisions on most key issues emanate from London. The constituent units of Northern Ireland, Scotland, and Wales ultimately take direction from the central government. An independent Parliament in Scotland may or may not provide a kind of release valve for simmering tensions with London. This simplifies realities somewhat, but ultimately direction is from the centre. New Zealand is perhaps the prime example of a unitary state based on the British model. A unitary model may work well with a fairly singular culture and a small population (New Zealand has about the same number of citizens as British Columbia).

2. The House of Commons

There are three essential prongs in the evolution of Canada's political system: The House of Commons and Senate, The Courts as interpreters of Law (especially since adoption of the Constitution Act, 1982), and the provinces and territories. The perpetual problem in Canadian politics is that a parliamentary system (unitary) does not co-exist well with a federal system (division of powers), particularly when the individual units exercise extraordinary powers of their own. Most of these powers are explicitly outlined in the Constitution Act, 1867, and the Constitution Act, 1982 (Natural Resources in 92A, for example). Any presumptive roles for the Queen, Governor General, and Lieutenant Governors have long been spent and are non-existent in Canada.

Even the role of Parliament has evolved in ways unforeseen by the Founders. House of Commons members take their cues from their leaders. This is particularly true of the governing party. The Prime Minister and the Cabinet exercise overarching iron clad power in this system. Powers embedded in the Prime Minister's Office (political appointees) and the Privy Council Office (permanent civil servants often seconded from other departments) are central to the operation of the Canadian Government.

Backbenchers have tended to become mere readers of speaking points in many cases. The daily forty- five minute Question Period is more about harassment and bickering than performing an informative function for the Canadian people. Members are allowed to read their pre-canned questions. Perhaps parliamentary procedure could learn something from the motion picture Academy Awards, which finally banned reading speeches in 2013. As well, House of Commons committees have rarely performed the kind of informative role intended, as membership on each committee is controlled by the majority party. Any important matter is addressed and decided by the Prime Minister and Cabinet.

Of course, this has totally undermined the concept of Parliamentary Supremacy. Citizens cannot be well-represented when a small cabal of elected and non-elected individuals drive the system. This underscores the "dysfunctionality" of Canada's central institution of government.

Just as important, Harper's Conservative government has totally undermined the role of the House of Commons. They exercised prorogation twice (2008-09) to avoid non-confidence votes. And the additional insult is that Parliament sat under one hundred days in 2006, 2008, and 2011, well below historic averages.

Harper has also forced through the House of Commons so-called omnibus bills in which unrelated matters are contained in one large bill. This is exactly the kind of thing that happens in the US Congress when "pork barrel" items are included in legislation that is totally unrelated to such items. It is little wonder that a recent Harris Decima poll showed that 84% of Canadians want more rules placed on the Prime Minister and Premiers as a means of increasing accountability and restricting cabinet unilateral action. The UK, Australia, and New Zealand have developed cabinet manuals which clarify rules, making their systems more accountable to citizens and clarifying the conditions under which non-confidence votes can take place.

Where is the accountability of Parliament to the citizens of Canada under this system? Responsible government has come to mean backbenchers are responsible to their Cabinet or Shadow Cabinet, and not the people of Canada. How this can be called democracy is beyond fathoming. Canada's Parliament is based on a conflictual system, but now treats opponents as enemies.

Canada's Cabinet system of government has resulted in an expedited legislative approval process at the expense of a fair vetting of proposed legislation. Forcing legislation through at will without appropriate review by all MPs can lead to draconian results.For example, recent regulatory changes to Employment Insurance allow regulators to knock on EI recipients' places of residence and question them on how they are pursuing job opportunities. Upper managers have been offered bonuses for cutting more people out of the system. This is a modern, if not violent, form of Gestapo tactics, or, the kind of harassment that the East German secret service engaged in. And it is hard to imagine how the purchase of the American built F-35 jet would have passed with a proper analysis of its durability and cost, which could have been done in House committees. Canada has had to back away in embarrassment, even as all F-35s have been grounded in the States due to engine faults.

What all of this attempts to demonstrate is that Canada's Parliamentary system is a cacophony of adversarial interests in which the majority party wins on every issue, whether or not they are supported by the true will of Canadians. How can such a system be sustained through time?

Michael Ignatieff, former leader of the Liberal Party, made this point and went further: What we have now is: : "...a hollowed-out democracy, which solitary politicians hurl abuse at each other in an empty chamber, and power accrues ever more steadily to the Prime Minister, Supreme Court, to the bureaucracy and to the press. And all of them regard the people elected to represent the people with contempt and derision."[1] Samara released a research paper in December, 2012, which found that only 36% of Canadians are satisfied with the performance of their MPs.[2]

3. **The Senate**

The Supremacy of Parliament also presumes a secondary place for the Senate, just as the House of Lords in the United Kingdom almost always takes its cues from the Parliament. Parliament is an elected body whereas the Senate is totally appointed by the Prime Minister. Efforts at constitutional reform of the Senate undermine Parliament and the Office of the Prime Minister. An elected, equal, and effective Senate would move Canada quickly to some form of Presidential system, much more like the US than the British system. And this is why Triple-E was really only intended to be Double-E: equal and elected, with constricted powers. The Triple-E concept was always perpetrated on Western Canada as part of, "We want in."[3] It was a myth from the start.

As well, such a move would undermine the role of Premiers and provincial governments as the centres of power really would likely return to Ottawa. A renewed credibility would focus on central Canada rather than the provinces. An elected Senate and Presidency have far-reaching consequences for a federation. Even though the tenth amendment to the US Constitution specifies that powers not given to the federal government belong to the states and the people, the political and judicial evolution of that system has blatantly placed the focus and eyes on Washington. Supreme Court decisions in the US pertaining to such matters as the Interstate Commerce Clause have further augmented federal power relative to the states. None of this has gone unnoticed in provinces such as Alberta, BC, and Quebec

The most obvious federal-provincial action pertaining to the Canadian Senate is the change to the Constitution Act, 1982, providing for a "suspensive veto" over constitutional changes in the House of Commons. The suspensive veto only stalls amendments for 180 days. This enshrines in the Constitution a castrated Senate rather than an effective one. Even though the Senate can still amend, stall, or simply ignore House of Commons legislation, that the Senate lacks power over any possible amendments to the Constitution is clearly an indicator of a truncated Senate. This has consolidated power in the House of Commons and, inter alia, in the Office of the Prime Minister and Cabinet.

No such limits are contained in the original BNA Act, 1867. The implication of the Supremacy of Parliament is clearly included(Peace, Order, Good Government), but the Senate had totally equal powers and legislation assented to by the Senate must be identical to what is passed by the House of Commons before being signed off by the Prime Minister. Now the Senate actually has *less* power than before, because of the 1982 limits on amendments to the Constitution.

This limiting constraint on the Senate exudes the real intent of the Prime Minister and Premiers: executive federalism. Executive federalism entails that all meaningful domestic matters involving fiscal transfers, overlap, joint jurisdiction or duplication require the advice and consent of both orders of government. The Senate is essentially a rubber stamp institution, filled with political appointees that are expected to facilitate, rather than deliberate, within the Canadian political process. Many appointed Senators do not take their role seriously, avoid attendance and are seriously abusing their spending accounts, as ongoing allegations contend. The late 2013 removal of three Senators from the Chamber is informative (Senators Brazeau, Duffy, and Wallin). The latter two were known to most Canadians as popular newscasters.

It is no surprise, then, that at least one Canadian political party has called for the elimination of the Senate: the New Democrat Party. The argument is that if the Senate does not really have a mandate to exercise its on paper responsibilities, then it might as well be taken out of the Constitution. Proponents of the Senate might argue that Senators indeed do exercise responsibilities related to editing bills and doing various committee investigations. The problem with the argument to abolish the Senate is that Canada would then no longer have institutions similar to those in the United Kingdom and the implications for federalism and the role of provinces and territories would certainly be muddied.

The counter argument would be that Canada never has had political institutions similar to Britain. The overwhelming responsibilities that have accrued to the provinces since the 1867 founding of this country have superseded any notion of having a system based on a centrist, parliamentary system of government.

Like Canada, the US divides responsibilities between the constituent units (states) and the federal government in Washington. The original intention articulated in the Articles of Confederation was to have a very loose Confederation where few powers would devolve to the central government. Hamilton and others argued against this position as it would lead to no national bank, customs duties and tariffs at state borders, separate currencies, etc.It became clear that if the US was to develop as one internally, and fend off any potential enemies externally, then more involvement from the central government would be required.

Suspicions by US founders like Madison, Adams, and Jefferson led to compromises that would create a union, yet divide responsibilities so that the US would never end up with a King George III. The consequence was a federal system founded in 1789 on limited government. It is a check and balance system where Presidential, Congressional, and Judicial powers are all limited (the President has a veto, judicial appointments are subject to Senate approval and Congress must pass all legislation in identical form). It is a separation of powers system among the President, Congress (the House of Representatives and the Senate), and the Judiciary.

The President and Vice-President are elected through an arcane Electoral College system where states ultimately determine the method of selection. Fears of true election by the population conditioned the Founders' thinking. Aristocracy still existed and was pervasive. So much for democracy based on "of, by and for the people". US Senators were appointed, and not elected by the people, until 1919. Oregon was the first state to elect its Senators and supported the right of women to vote, and continues to this day to be one of the most progressive states in the US. For example, it lead in development of the euthanasia or right to die law.

The US Judiciary is also outlined in the Constitution. Its role became perfectly clarified in Marbury vs. Madison: Acts of Congress, even if signed by the President, are subject to judicial review. The Rule of Law is supreme. Conversely, unitary parliamentary systems place ultimate trust in an elected parliament, hence the Supremacy of Parliament. Dicey, the preeminent expert on British constitutional law, said that, "Parliament… has the right to make or unmake any law whatsoever and no other constitutional body can override it."[4]

4. The Provinces

Canada's constitution recognizes the Supremacy of Parliament, yet explicitly outlines a long list of powers which belong exclusively to the provinces. These are mainly outlined in (s.92 and s.93) of the Constitution Act, 1867, and then there are joint areas of jurisdiction, including agriculture, immigration (s.95), and the Canada Pension Plan (s.95A).

Natural resources belong to the provinces, although Alberta and Saskatchewan did not gain control of these until 1930. And even then, the implementation of the National Energy Program in 1980 and previous measures that effectively confiscated perhaps hundreds of billions of oil dollars from the province of Alberta with a two price policy (domestic and international), proved that Western provinces only had limited jurisdiction over resources. Such unilateral federal action was eliminated with the passage (s.92A) of the Constitution Act, 1982.

It was not the intention of the Founders that provinces would exercise control over what have become the largest governmental spending areas of health, education and social services, and such significant revenue makers as oil, natural gas, coal, lumber, potash, uranium, diamonds, gold etc. No one could have imagined the extent and scope of the modern welfare state. History, then, has played out shockingly differently than any group of political thinkers at the time could have imagined. Even extraordinary powers of clairvoyance could not have shed luminance on the political future of Canada.

While most provinces clearly lack the fiscal revenues and capacity to carry out successfully their social program laden responsibilities, their ability to carry them out at all with limited or no federal interference attests to their powerful role in this system. To be sure, the federal government in the 1980s and 1990s attempted to press for an increased presence in health, education, and such other areas as manpower training. The passage of the Canada Health Act (1980) is perhaps the most blatant example.

The very existence of the Canadian Institute for Health Information (CIHI) is another. An interprovincial/territorial body would be quite capable of exercising such functions as determining the success or lack thereof of health care systems. Certainly, the providers of health care are in a much better position to develop measuring techniques than a remote, disconnected Ottawa.

And the federal government has been able to interject itself into education with direct scholarships to students, thus bypassing the provinces. Quebec, especially, has been concerned about such intrusions into its exclusive jurisdiction and in the early 1950s enacted a provincial income tax to circumvent Ottawa's incursions into post-secondary education.

During the 1990s, the federal government attempted to usurp provincial powers through a series of actions that may be referred to as "administrative federalism." In 1999, all provinces except Quebec, agreed to a social union agreement entitled, "A Framework to Improve the Social Union for Canadians." It is ironic that provinces took the initiative to develop the social union concept yet the federal government was able to turn an interprovincial initiative into a federal-provincial one that would have the potential to lead into a new era of intrusiveness into areas of exclusive provincial jurisdiction. The blurring of responsibilities through "partnerships" and joint program development is yet another example of system dysfunction in Canada's political system as the federal government was attempting to use its spending power to have its way with the provinces.

In many ways, however, the provinces actually have more control over the Canadian economic and political system than Ottawa. Their jurisdiction is constitutional and their spending powers are extensive. As well, their powers to borrow would make their southern state neighbours envious.

Contrast the intent of the Canadian founders with their US counterparts. The former clearly intended a centralized system, where the central features of banking, interprovincial commerce and the military, would be within their scope. Their eyes were focused on the US, where the divisions in the North and South were seen as a consequence of too much decentralization. Ironically, the delineation of responsibilities empowered provinces and resulted in an upside down effect: A centralized intent has evolved into a decentralized result.

Conversely, the US founders envisioned a decentralized system where most powers would devolve to the states and the people. But as a result of court cases involving key aspects, such as the Interstate Commerce Clause, the US is much more centralized in its decision-making process than Canada. Add on a President elected by the people and an elected Senate and it is no wonder that almost exclusive attention is directed toward the Washington Beltway. The upside down effect is once again the result. The Government of Canada would no doubt relish and envy the prospect of such US powers. Power is an aphrodisiac to politicians just as sensuality is, ideally, to the rest of us.

To be sure, the fiscal powers of Ottawa, combined with exclusive Bank of Canada control over monetary policy, offer significant leverage in governing capacity. To determine interest rates exclusively gives the Bank of Canada, or the Bank of England for that matter, powers not conceivably imaginable by the likes of Hobbes, Locke, or even Hamilton. The Bank of Canada and the Federal Reserve in the US exercise independence and almost god-like powers over monetary matters that must make Prime Ministers and Presidents envious!

Even though the federal government has unlimited power to raise revenue through various means, including federal income tax, corporate income tax, the Goods and Services Tax, tariffs and customs duties, and so on, provinces also have access to unlimited direct forms of taxation. And the bulk of spending in the Canadian federation is exercised by the provinces and territories.

An elected Senate and Presidency has far-reaching consequences for a federation. Even though the 10th amendment to the US Constitution specifies that powers not given to the federal government belong to the states and the people, the political and judicial evolution of that system has blatantly placed the focus and eyes on Washington and not the states. US federal power, such as interpretations of the Interstate Commerce Clause has further centralized power in the capital. Evolution toward a US style Presidential system in Canada is highly unlikely as provinces would not want to lose any powers. And, in any case, the American system suffers from perpetual gridlock; its checks and balances system is not leading to decisive decision-making. Its system only works at the last minute in a novel form of crisis decision-making.

Such a move would undermine the role of Premiers and provincial governments as the centres of power really would return to Ottawa. A renewed credibility would focus on central decision-making. This has never gone unnoticed by Premiers, particularly key players such as Quebec, Ontario and Alberta.

5. The Judiciary

Until recent Canadian judicial history, appointed judges were not to override the will of the elected representatives of the people. It was a combination of the Statute of Westminster, 1931, and the Judiciary Act of 1949 that really created an independent Canadian State and an independent judiciary. The Statute of Westminster essentially declared that Canadian acts in conflict with British law would prevail (the statute also affected other commonwealth countries including Australia, New Zealand and South Africa). The Judiciary Act, 1949, established the independence of Canada's legal system from that of the United Kingdom. This established the independence of the Supreme Court of Canada.

But the Court tended to be more tentative in its decisions, unlike the British Court which, in some cases, had widely extended provincial powers in the 1930s by narrowing the breadth of the residual clause (Peace, Order and Good Government) and the trade and commerce clause in s.91(2). However, assenting to the constitutionality of the National Energy Program and the Goods and Services Tax, which were fiercely opposed by Alberta, significantly undermined provincial powers.

The advent of The Charter of Rights and Freedoms in the Constitution Act, 1982, changed an entire dimension of Canadian politics and was a harbinger of judicial activism. Not even the Warren Supreme Court in the U.S would venture into such unchartered legal territory. No longer would it be up to the federal government or provinces to enhance or usurp the rights of its citizens. Now the Court would play that role, and it has done so vigorously, with or without the support of governments. This has been a fundamental game changer to the very notion of Parliamentary Supremacy of both orders of government, federal and provincial.

Arguments were made prior to adoption of the Charter that enshrining such a document in the Constitution would be redundant, as the federal government had long before passed its own Human Rights Act in 1960 and several provinces had followed suit, including Ontario (1962) and Alberta (1971). Prime Minister Trudeau was persistent in his dream of imprinting legal and other rights into the Constitution, arguing that no government should be able to take inalienable rights away. Alberta, British Columbia, Saskatchewan, and Manitoba were concerned about how an increase in judicial powers to decide cases would affect their powers. Clearly, the powers of the federal government and the provinces would be diminished if courts decided to occupy the vacuum and fill it with their unelected judicial decisions. And that is exactly what they have done. The forces favouring the sanctity of citizens' individual rights were contending with traditional notions of Parliamentary Sovereignty and quite clearly the former won that war. Within a blink of an eye, Canada's system of governance had moved closer to the US style. No longer could Canadian governments be the ultimate determiner on hot button social issues such as abortion, capital punishment, euthanasia etc.

The Morganthaler Abortion Case is far-ranging and essentially legalizes abortion up to the point of delivery.[5] Roe v. Wade (1973) in the US is much more constrained and only allows a woman to control her destiny in the first trimester. The key point is that neither in Canada nor the US can legislators overturn the determined will of the courts. Parliamentary Supremacy equals court supremacy.

Perhaps even more disturbing, courts now have the power to dictate what governments would be required to do in the critical fields of health, education, and welfare. The November 2012 Supreme Court case (Moore v British Columbia Education SCC61) establishes the right of all students to an equal education whether the student suffers dyslexia, autism, or any other special needs situation.[6] The Court awarded Jeffrey Moore's family $100,000 in remuneration for monies incurred in private schools to compensate for what he did not receive in the public school system.

Governments' fiscal constraints are no longer a reason to deny the supremacy of citizens' rights. That the budgetary cupboard is bare is no longer an argument to limit the promises of governments. One can imagine the implications for health care in Canada. The guarantees of universality, accessibility, public administration, portability, and comprehensiveness could all be refashioned and redesigned through the court system. To the extent that Canadians identify health care as their most important characteristic as a nation, it is likely that courts will explore the meaning of these conditions to the fullest extent in the future.

Court decisions of this magnitude are far-reaching and far beyond the capability of governments to satisfy. This provides further evidence of dysfunction in Canada's institutions. The judicial prong of these institutions is undoing the original idea of Parliamentary Supremacy.

6. Conclusions

Political history evolves in unfathomable and unpredictable ways. Both Canada and the US have undergone a metamorphosis every bit as extreme as nature's muse: the move from larvae, to cocoon, to butterfly .The Founder's thinking has been turned upside down in both Canada and the US: from centralization to decentralization in the former and the opposite in the latter. Centrifugal forces have generally prevailed since the 1960s in Canada, although provinces have never had the wherewithal to exercise their responsibilities adequately. This adds to the general malaise. And the federal government has certainly sought a greater role through its ever present exercise of the spending power. This is its Trojan horse and it has a certain resonance with the people.

All of Canada's political institutions are dysfunctional; they do not harmonize in sync like a well-built motor vehicle. Dysfunction abounds: from the dwindling role of the House of Commons, to the unelected Senate, to the new, powerful role of the Judiciary, to the powerful Prime Minister in a majority government, a silenced concept of Responsible Government, to the constant acrimony between the federal government and provinces.

The state of the federation is not healthy or sustainable.

Chapter 6
Intergovernmental Situations

A federation can only survive if there is some semblance of harmony between both the national government and the constituent units, as well as amongst the units themselves. This chapter, which is on federal-provincial fiscal transfer relations, will explainthe severe stresses within the Canadian confederation pertaining to the lack of adequate transfers for the provinces to carry out their constitutionally mandated responsibilities properly. This chapter considers the situations of provinces and the relations among the units and whether they contribute to sustaining the Canadian union or are facilitating its demise.

1. Quebec

In discussing intergovernmental affairs, there is no better place to start than with the situation in Quebec. Two referenda have been held in that province to separate from Canada, in 1980 and 1995. Only a massive campaign blitz within the province kept Quebec in the federation in the last referendum. Sooner or later, the province will once again have a Parti Quebecois (PQ) Government in power committed to independence. A third referendum is likely to happen during that government's mandate. What are the implications for the remainder of Canada?

Donald Savoie wrote a very sensitive and pertinent note in the Globe and Mail on June 29, 2012, warning that Quebec federalists, those committed to a one Canada concept, may find themselves alone in the next referendum.[1] It is unlikely that Canadians will rush to Montreal and Quebec City to proclaim their need to keep Quebec in. The West, as Savoie contends, can fly solo. Ontario has become much more insular, partly due to the recession and partly due to its becoming an equalization-receiving province that contends, rightfully, that it has put much more out than it has received in fiscal transfers. The Maritimes and Newfoundland have their own serious issues with Quebec and are hardly great supporters of Quebec's ambitions.

As Quebec is not a party to the Constitution Act 1982, the Canadian angst continues. In Jamaica, they have a saying: They do not have problems; they have situations. Well, the great Canadian Union situation is unprecedented. Quebec is forced to abide by a constitution its legitimate government in 1982 never agreed to, and no other one since then has agreed either through legislative assembly decisions or a referendum. In fact, successive Quebec governments, PQ and Liberal, have utilized s.33, the Notwithstanding Clause, to opt out of any federal legislation affecting their interests and falling within the appropriate Charter of Rights sections, 1 and 7-15.[2]

Efforts in 1987 (Meech Lake Accord) and 1992 (Charlottetown Accord) were utter failures. Both were driven by the elites in the federal and provincial governments, but Canadians were confused, suspicious, and skeptical. Charlottetown was a convoluted mix of this and that, and many direct participants in the process even voted against what they had wrought. What sometimes used to pass as "elite accommodation" or grand accommodative decisions is no longer possible. What has been called "executive federalism" no longer has credibility in this country, even if good chunks of daily intergovernmental business are certainly based, and dependent, upon it.

In June 2012, Ipsos Reid released a poll which is telling. 49% of Canadians outside of Quebec agreed that if the province separates, it is not really a big deal. And 27% of Albertans supported separating from Canada. 31% of all Canadians in the sample said that they really did not care if any province separated.[3] These numbers are shocking. A general indifference toward the future of Canada has settled in. Have the citizens of specific provinces or regions become numb to Quebec's demands? Has a palpable weariness and insularity set in?

Certainly since 1980, Quebecers have had one foot in Canada and one outside of it. As long as they can wrestle more and more money out of Ottawa, they are in. When they feel short-changed, they are out. This is called "profitable federalism."[4] No other jurisdiction has quite looked at Canada as a country that depends solely upon what it gets out of it rather than a sense of belonging to a greater project. And it does not seem to matter if the government in power is PQ or Liberal. Most Quebecers are quite indifferent to the interests in the West, or even Ontario, for that matter.

Ironically, there is a keen awareness amongst the business and government and intellectual elites about the need to speak English to trade with the US This, of course, contradicts French only or French first language laws in the province. It is truly disenchanting that English speakers in provinces outside of Quebec are more likely to receive more amicable service in restaurants in places like Quebec City if they say they are from the US rather than Ontario, for example. It is similar to Americans wearing Canadian flags on their lapels in Paris!

Sovereignty Governance is the new rallying cry of Quebec's last premier, Marois. There is little new on the agenda: greater control over labour market responsibilities and money, more language signs only in French, and , generally, more efforts to disengage from Ottawa and the provinces. Symbolically, and perhaps foolishly, Quebec purportedly had decided to speak at all federal-provincial meetings only in French; optional at the cocktail parties, lunches, and dinners during these gatherings. The costs of translating the many hundreds of meetings from officials up to Ministers would be prohibitive. In the extraordinarily unlikely event that this policy proceeds in the future, Quebec may well end up talking to itself.

2. Alberta, BC, Saskatchewan (ABC'S)

Albertans perceive federation from a totally different perspective. Coming into confederation in 1905, it took a mere thirty or so years for the province to engage in political and economic legislative activities no other province has since. The province set up its own bank, printed its own coinage and engaged in a number of other activities to fight off the worst effects of the depression. Alberta Treasury Branches thrive to this day. Not content with the designation "hewers of wood and drawers of water," the province was rebellious, cantankerous, and intent on carving its own destiny. Too many farmers had lost their homes to the banks in Toronto and Montreal during the Great Depression. Partial natural resource ownership was not even granted to Alberta and Saskatchewan until 1930, and it was not until the discovery of oil in Leduc in 1947 that the province began to perceive the possibilities of its own future economic destiny.

While reviled and certainly scoffed at as the bible thumping province, particularly under Premiers Aberhart and Manning, the province partly transformed itself with the election of Premier Lougheed in 1970.Conservative values still dominated (religion, small government, self-reliance) but a new, more cosmopolitan, outlook took the reign of power. The first act of the new government was a bill of rights. The same party remains in power to this day, after 43 years. There is little or nothing that temporal, ex-Premier Redford would share in common with earlier premiers, and her views, and those of her morphed party, are arguably to the left of Lougheed's Progressive Conservative Party. Opposition leader, Danielle Smith, of the Wild Rose Party, is clearly in touch with a significant portion of the Alberta population that would reverse any moves toward a more cosmopolitan, progressive province. It would certainly become more insular and feisty with Ottawa.

The massive inflows of Canadians from other provinces, as well as immigrants from other countries, have certainly had an impact on the politics of the province. Conversely, there has also been a rub-off effect on these same newcomers. Whether they come from Ontario,

Newfoundland, BC, the US, Asia, or elsewhere, a surprising blending in and acceptance of Albertan basic values often prevails quickly in their political and economic thinking. Materialism and individual well-being are powerful elixirs that drive these perspectives. No other province would so thoroughly embrace Ayn Rand's philosophical thinking as Alberta would,[5] but there is a certain generosity that also touches the spirit of this province and is most evident in the enormous, forced indirect economic intergovernmental outflows from Alberta taxpayers.

The impact of decisions in the East on Alberta farmers in the 30s, the NEP and related federal decisions during this period affecting the oil and natural gas industry, the unequal application of fiscal transfers, the attempted unilateral imposition of changes to the BNA ACT, and the imposition of the Goods and Services Tax have all taken their toll on Alberta's perspective on federal-provincial and intergovernmental relations. There is an old cliché which is as relevant today as ever: there is nothing wrong with being paranoid if there really is something to fear. In the case of Alberta, there was an obvious attempt to usurp its natural resource rents in 1980. The consequent bellicosity of the Alberta Government is certainly understandable. Realities could not be denied: Alberta was not going to be able to obtain world prices for its natural resources, even as Ontario and Quebec were realizing world prices for their manufacturing industries (principally autos and car parts). The West would be permanent hewers of wood and drawers of water (non-manufacturing), and while wheat, oats, canola etc. would receive world prices, oil and natural gas would somehow be treated differently domestically.

Premier Lougheed essentially said on TV in 1980 that the province had ushered the federal government out of its house and was seriously thinking of kicking them off the porch! The Lougheed name was steeped deeply in the Canadian Pacific Railway and the financial industry and Canadiana, so this was quite the statement for this period of Canadian political history. It was not hyperbole. And it was not desperation. It was exasperation; the culmination of a federal government process that clearly discriminated against Alberta relative to any other province. Albertans were thinking of going it alone.It was not unnoticed in academia that an independent Alberta would have rivaled any of the 'Sheik' fiefdoms in wealth, and yet maintains its democratic principles. Albertans were indeed castigated as "blue-eyed Arabs."

The province could become the envy of the world, except that the 1982 world recession dramatically changed the landscape. Oil prices collapsed. From Calgary to Fort McMurray, jobs and the dreams of untold families were lost. Bumper stickers declared: "Oh God, please let there be another oil boom; I promise not to piss it away this time!" There was no longer a federal government impetus for a National Energy Program and related efforts to confiscate Alberta's wealth.And they duly undid the unfair and discriminatory acts.

In 2001, an open letter, signed by then Alliance leader Harper and five others, was sent to Premier Klein calling for a 'fire wall' against Ottawa.[6] It would include collecting its own income tax, its own police forces (no RCMP), an independent pension plan disconnected from the CPP, and a greater role in immigration. All of these items have already been achieved in Quebec, so none of this is particularly revolutionary. Even Ontario has its own Provincial Police (OPP). Premier Klein struck a committee to investigate the possibilities, but nothing changed. Clearly, the thinking in Edmonton and Calgary was disconnected from more radical thinking in the rural communities that would have willingly and widely endorsed such notions.

It is not only thinking in various political communities that always counts in moving governments. MLA's (members of the legislative assembly) absolutely listen to their constituent interests. Their political survival depends upon it. Cabinet decisions in Alberta are certainly affected by what constituents are telling their elected members. This is grass roots democracy and manifestly affects the dialogue.

Nonetheless, there is an established, entrenched civil service in the province that also touches and affects decisions in very dramatic ways. At the highest levels, staff departments never really supported rural interest perspectives, or even those of Calgarians. Such departments would include Finance and Intergovernmental Affairs, but would also include personnel in Health, Education, Justice, Social Services, Labour, etc. It is a matter of conjecture as to why this is the case, but the fact that so many of the recruits in management within the Alberta civil service have come from the East is telling. They have brought their political visions with them and none of those perspectives ever included the possibility of disengagement, as their Ontario born, one-Canada at all costs "print" has perhaps obfuscated a coherent western ideological picture.

This could largely explain why Alberta has never pressed very hard for a tax point transfer, for example. Such a transfer would secure for Albertans some concept of stability in what they would get back in health, education, and social services from the government versus what they have paid in via personal, corporate and a myriad of other taxes. The government closest to its people should be doing the taxing and spending in the major, core social program fields for which they are constitutionally responsible. Only a tax point transfer ultimately accomplishes this objective. Other benefits include greater transparency and accountability to tax-paying citizens in Alberta.

A closer relation between raising revenue and spending it would go some distance in mitigating western alienation. The feeling that the western provinces are being cheated in what they get in fiscal transfers relative to what they put in could no longer be a legitimate rationale. A one-time tax transfer, similar to the EPF tax transfer in 1976-77, and appropriately adjusted to account for current spending in the major spending envelopes, would reduce dramatically the current acrimonious relations between the federal government and the West.

It has been noted that it is unlikely, if not impossible, that any federal government in the foreseeable future would concur with such a proposal. Governments do not easily cede control of portions of the financial purse, even if the Canadian government essentially wrested away from the provinces such tax room during the Second World War in tax rental agreements. More tax spending ability means more visibility for the federal government; spending gains credit; credit leads to more votes in ridings throughout the land. Perhaps an equally important point is that increased access to taxpayer dollars could lead to greater disengagement from the Canadian union, or even independence given the appropriate conditions. Successive analysts in the PCO and PMO in Ottawa under different administrations have not been blind to this possibility.

British Columbia is a difficult province to decipher in its intra and intergovernmental relations. Internally, like Alberta, the province splits along urban and rural lines: the urban centres being more cosmopolitan, catholic, and liberal in their views. Rural BC, except for a few outlier regions and ridings due to traditional, historical, and mainly rail and coal union influences, is almost identical to Alberta in political philosophies. A suspicion of government in general, a reluctance to change political views toward such issues as gay marriage, equality rights for women, and a semi-demonization of the Vancouver region, is all part of the perspective. Even growing interior cities, like Kelowna, Kamloops, and Penticton, hold tightly to traditional conservative values. This is probably likely to change with growing influxes of people from central Canada, Vancouver, and immigrants.

In its intergovernmental relations, BC has often seemed disengaged. Relative to its economic size, it has not been a major player in discussions involving federal transfers, health matters, labour and social issues etc. Some of this is undoubtedly due to conscious decisions on the part of successive BC governments, Social Credit, NDP and Liberal, to focus on internal BC matters rather than the intergovernmental venue. This preoccupation with intra-provincial matters can putatively be explained by the continuing civil internecine squabbling and political conflict within the province. There is no consensus in BC except that the province is called " Super NaturalBeautiful British Columbia" and that indeed it is on the west side of the Rockies! It is no understatement to suggest that BC has not been a driver of provincial interests within Confederation in recent history.

That the province is a continuing ideological battle field between an exaggerated left and right explains its singularity and insularity relative to Alberta. There is never total certainty about who will win the next election. The strength of unions, teachers, nurses etc. in BC provides an ample adversarial counter to the large and small business interests within the province, which themselves, do not necessarily speak with one voice. Internally, the citizens of BC have political imagination and will turn with vengeance on the party in power when they think that wrong doing has gone on or that they have been served badly. Taking over from Premier Campbell of the Liberal Party, Premier Clark has found nothing but grief with the foundered Harmonized Sales Tax (Combined Goods and Services Tax and Provincial Sales Tax) battle, and internal corruption issues involving civil servants spending public monies to support the party's re-election. The pattern continues. Incessant focus on the internal has undermined any credible intergovernmental presence for BC for the foreseeable future.

Ironically, the land locked province of Saskatchewan has been more open to an intergovernmental presence and broader vision within Canada. As previously noted, it was Tommy Douglas and his Cabinet that would move Canada forward with universal health care, beginning in his province in 1965. The idea caught on like wildfire and was quickly embraced as a federal concept soon after, universally adopted in every province by 1968 and it is not surprising that Alberta was the last holdout. What accounts for the more compassionate, Trans-Canada, vision of the country relative to its neighbours to the West? One cannot look to the original composition of immigrants, say in Saskatchewan and Alberta, and find answers. Both were based on agriculture, and the newcomers came from all over Europe. Both also have a significant Ukrainian population. How is it possible for the province to elect Cooperative Commonwealth Federation and NDP governments while Alberta has persistently leaned right with Social Credit and Conservative governments?

Certainly, the massive influx of immigrants from Texas, Oklahoma and other oil-producing areas within the US has had a significant impact on the ideology within Alberta. Saskatchewan's more recent development of heavy oil extraction and natural gas exploration are having an impact on its significant inflow of immigrants from Alberta and elsewhere. Oil executives, electricians, welders, and pipefitters have all carried their political values with them. This could partly explain the more recent tilt toward support for the Conservative government of Premier Wall. Perhaps symbolically, the city of Lloydminster, straddling both sides of the Alberta and Saskatchewan border, ties these two provinces together as a pair of reluctant twins. Both entered Confederation in 1905. Albertans access health care on the Saskatchewan side as that is where the hospital is located. Regular renewal of interprovincial agreements secures such access and payment for services.

In April 2010, BC, Alberta, and Saskatchewan formed the New West Partnership.[7] The implications of this partnership could be significant, if not shocking Canada-wide. Alberta is now pressing hard for a nation-wide free trade agreement. The Partnership Agreement purports to establish: "Canada's largest open, efficient, and stable market and creates a framework for on-going cooperation to strengthen our economy... and expand our presence around the world." What makes this agreement remarkable is that it is the first serious attempt to liberalize interprovincial trade, investment, and labour mobility within the country. Each province agrees not to subsidize its own industries or citizens at the expense of the other two. Labour market mobility is to be universally recognized; trades recognized in BC are recognized in Saskatchewan. A plumber is a plumber; a Medical Office Assistant is the same in each province. Procurement policies would be non-discriminatory except for nominal amounts (purchases by governments). Even dispute settlement mechanisms, when parties do not agree on the rules, will be established. Some of this is based on and emulated from the free trade agreement between Canada, the US, and Mexico.

"We are stronger as one than if we stand apart. With one voice, the West will be a leader on issues that are vital to the nation's competiveness," declared the three Premiers.[8] This is a significant deal in that it essentially calls for a free trade zone in the West realizing the free movement of investment, goods, services and labour. There is no parallel agreement anywhere else in Canada: a bricklayer mason in Ontario cannot lay bricks in Quebec.

One other poignant aspect to this agreement deserves note. Manitoba is no longer considered to be part of the West. This is a basic abrogation of the Western Premier's Conference which includes Manitoba as well as the other three. The reasons for Manitoba's exclusion are a matter of conjecture but at least two reasons are suggestive: 1) Its politics are different than the others; it has an NDP government whereas the others are all conservative (Liberal in BC means conservative); 2) There is a recognition that the economy in Manitoba is more congruent with that of Ontario than the West. Whether the Partnership can withstand political changes in BC or Saskatchewan to the NDP is uncertain. Politics definitely conditions fraternity. Alberta is the only province in the four western provinces that will remain within the conservative spectrum for the foreseeable future, even with an NDP government. The populist Rachel Notley, the new Premier, is still a great supporter of the oil industry.

3. Ontario

Due to the severe recession in 2009, Ontario has undergone a major transformation from a "have" province to a "have not". Over reliance on moving automobiles, auto parts, and other manufactured goods through Detroit and elsewhere has no doubt contributed to the malaise. In federal Ottawa and in Queens Park, Toronto, it was unthinkable that the driving engine of Canada since Confederation would fall on hard times. In fact, in a previous recession in the early nineteen eighties, Ontario became eligible for equalization payments, and the Department of Finance re-configured the formula, as they have done so often, to ensure that Ontario would not receive such payments: It had a higher average per capita income than the other provinces, and this was considered sufficient to deny payments.

But now its fiscal capacity has been diminished and it does receive significant equalization payments to bring it up to the average of other provinces. Putative fiscal capacity, arbitrarily determined ultimately, and in an authoritative fashion, by the federal government, is the only measure that is used to determine what would be necessary to provide comparable public services and similar rates of taxation throughout the land, as required in S.35 of the Constitution Act, 1982.

With a population of 13.5 million, and a robust industrial, technological and agricultural base, Ontario remains formidable economically and would be the envy of most countries in the world.It is indeed Central Canada, but it no longer has the respect or even attention of the West, except maybe for such specialty areas as investment banking. The drift of economic power has patently been Western. Examples include the unceasing and unending billions in investments in the Oil Sands of Alberta and the plush symbols of wealth in the contemporary high rises of Vancouver. It is almost as if there is a nascent transformative trade connection underway between the West and, say, Hong Kong, Shanghai, and Delhi.

The ties, artificial and real, that once bound Central Canada to the West have become threadbare. It is little consolation that the Maritimes are still very much dependent upon Ontario exports. Ontario has lost its way.

It is not only the decline in manufacturing and consequent incomes that is salient. The province has hitched its fortunes to the US When the North-Eastern US economy thrives, so does Ontario. It is no frivolous venture that the Ontario and federal government have lobbied hard for the new bridge across Detroit, the busiest in the world in terms of trade. It has even been prepared to finance most of it! That is how vital it is to its economic interests. Bottlenecks are slowing trade and profits.

The province, in intergovernmental venues, has not been particularly strong in its presence in recent history, often being outshone by the federal government, Quebec, Alberta, and even Saskatchewan and Newfoundland. Perhaps Canada's middle-kingdom assumed a forever dominance over economics and politics within the country. Eastern US rust belt states with a similar smug attitude have paid a severe price in an electoral sense, as well as standard of living for not modernizing their industries. Economic and political power has perceptively moved West and South. Complacency has resulted in massive emigration to where the jobs are located. Even more importantly, the North East has lost many Congressional seats to the engines of growth: California, Florida, Texas. A finite 435 Congressional Districts means reallocation to the population growth areas.

In a bizarre electoral twist, the number of seats in Canada never decreases and only increases with population. Such electoral foolery is entrenched in the Constitution Act, 1867. Ontario, instead of suffering the consequences of economic decline, is actually being rewarded with the bulk of new Members of Parliament in Ottawa! New immigration, rather than interprovincial migration, is the principal cause. Ontario will actually gain another 15 seats, adding to its current 106 for a total of 121, or 36% of all seats.

Can a country succeed when a province is being rewarded with enhanced electoral power even as it carries less and less fiscal weight within the federation? To the extent that economic situations determine political ones, it is anomalous that Ontario should be gaining political clout within the Union. Quite clearly, the Constitution and Elections Canada bear no relation whatsoever to basic economic realities. This is not to say that there is a legitimate rationale for an exact coincidence between population and economy, but the current situation is unsustainable over time. Yet, now Ontario vociferously complains about its lack of fiscal capacity to provide services to its citizens relative to other equalization-receiving provinces.

Can credible arguments be made that the province should receive a greater chunk of federal fiscal transfers (CHT, CST, Equalization) than it currently receives? The short answer is no. A recent paper produced by the Mowat centre contends that, "...all provinces (should) have the fiscal capacity to provide reasonably comparable levels of services at reasonably comparable levels of taxation...".[9] "Fiscal capacity" is being snuck in as the central criteria in determining payments for the major social programs and equalization. There is no mention of fiscal capacity anywhere in federal legislation or in the Constitution Act, 1982. While Equalization is based on averaging out major sources of revenues, and assigning provinces plusses and minuses relative to these sources, it is ultimately the federal government that jigs the figures to pay out what it is willing to pay and to whom these payments go to. The system is absolutely not based on fiscal capacity.

If it were so based, all of Alberta's natural resource revenues would be brought into the equation and would be equalized. Ottawa would go bankrupt!Equalization is intended to provide enough benefits to receiving provinces to deliver comparable services with comparable rates of taxation. Comparable does not mean identical. In fact, "comparable" is a nebulous concept which finance officials are ill-equipped to define. Perhaps it is a philosophical concept bearing little relation to fiscal capacity.

A further stretch from reality is the claim in the paper that Ontario contributed 39% of federal revenues but receives 34 percent of expenditures.[10] What is missing in this "reality" is that Alberta, for example, contributes at least twice per capita relative to what it receives back.[11]

While this paper is not a product of the Ontario Government, it is clearly in harmony with it. Ontario may be creating a situation that attempts to exploit the transfer system to its advantage. It is even argued in the paper that some provinces are "gaming" the system by underestimating revenue intakes from items like hydroelectricity rents. And what would be said about Alberta, which collects 0% from sales taxes as there is no sales tax in the province? This decreases its fiscal capacity severely.

Finally, it should be noted that natural resource revenues from oil, gas, and whatever else are one time extractions and cannot be replaced. Income from these sources cannot be treated the same way as cars and car parts and everything else that Ontario manufactures. While forests are renewable, oil is not. Treating one time extraction of natural resources the same as renewable manufacturing is extremely problematic. And it contributes to dividing Canadians rather than uniting them.

4. The Maritimes and Newfoundland

Nova Scotia, New Brunswick, and PEI tend to be complacent partners in Confederation. They are all extremely dependent upon Ottawa's transfer system and act accordingly. Once again, this shows the impact of economies on politics. Stagnant economies with no real natural resource wealth are not a recipe for strong provinces capable of challenging the federal government. New ship building in the greater Halifax area, and the proposed pipeline moving natural gas and oil from West to East will definitely add some dearly needed economic activity to New Brunswick and Nova Scotia.

Newfoundland is a different story as it has become a resource rich province for the foreseeable future. Even before this new- found oil wealth, the province has always had a spunky spirit, more like Alberta than anywhere else within Canada. Relations with Quebec have always been frosty at best. Quebec does not recognize Labrador as part of Newfoundland, and Quebec enticed Premier Joey Smallwood into a terrible deal to sell hydropower to the Northeastern states, which the province is locked into until 2031. This situation continues to evolve and fester, as Newfoundland will move its new hydro activity via cable to Nova Scotia with the assistance of federal loans and guarantees. Quebec, of course is arguing that these are subsidies. How much easier it could have been to move electricity over Quebec territory? Such is the situation. It does not bode well for a one Canada concept.

5. Situations (summary)

Major change is going on within Canada amongst the provinces. While the Quebec situation continues to garner the bulk of attention, it is no longer the sole source of concern. That the province did not sign onto the Constitution Act, 1982, and that no government since has agreed to it, is certainly indicative of a major failure in Canadian constitutional politics. Executive federalism, or decisions contrived by government elites, is no longer trusted to cut the compromising deals required for Canada to continue functioning as one polity. And when decisions were placed before Canadians in the Charlottetown Accord (again agreed to by the governmental elites), the people all over Canada turned it down. This ethereal condition or state of Canada does not auger well.

Even more disturbing is that no government within the Confederation wants to open up constitutional discussions again. Such talks seem to be a recipe of failure. But what are the alternatives? Apparently none! Governments carry on as if a country can be run when a key provincial government, Quebec, has not signed on to the major constitutional changes. The bitterness of this situation is palpable within Quebec, even in the English and Allophone communities. Canadians, in general, seem to be politically sleep-walking! Symbolic decisions by the ex-PQ government within Quebec to speak French only at intergovernmental venues may seem silly, but all jurisdictions should take notice. Quebec is becoming a non-participant, a reluctant attendee that knows it must tend to its own interests, which requires a presence and a speaking platform. Incipient, palpable, persistent political alienation is not indicative of an ongoing endeavour to grow a country. The Quebec situation seems intractable. It matters little which power, Liberal or PQ rules: the direction is the same.

In the West, the New Partnership Agreement would seem to show a possibility for a Canada united economically, if nothing else. After all, it calls for the removal of barriers to trade, mobility and movement of people and, ultimately, capital, among the three western provinces. Such an agreement, *inter alia*, would seem to be capable of being copied throughout the land. Will the players of BC, Alberta and Saskatchewan follow through on their commitments? Or will politics determine economics? Surely, Quebecers are definitely driven by the political scene, even as they vigorously pursue profitable federalism in the interim. Sequential changes in government are normal in B.C and Saskatchewan. The Liberal Party in BC and the Conservatives in Alberta and Saskatchewan share a general political conservative perspective. An NDP government in either BC or Saskatchewan could undermine previous decisions made. As facile as it may seem, political affiliation does affect the big picture in terms of economy. That Christy Clark, former Premier of BC, attempted to extract resource rents from Alberta if the pipeline to Kitimat or Prince Rupert were to proceed is indicative of how intra-provincial politics can affect rational decision-making anywhere. Electoral victory means everything within a province and supersedes intergovernmental economic sense!

Nonetheless, the partnership agreement is a powerful symbol of what the West is capable of doing to secure its future, and the possibility of a Western entity separate from Canada is not impossible, and is not going unnoticed.If nothing else, provinces should not necessarily be seen as individual entities, separate from their neighbours.

Ontario continues to remain a powerful force within the nation, economically and politically. It is no longer the middle-Kingdom, China style, but it still is the financial centre of Canada and its manufactured goods continue to move East to West and, more importantly for it, North to South. Its situation is much like California's. In good times it does very well; in bad times it suffers. It's awesome manufacturing, financial, and technological bases determine its future, and it will always be positive.Moreover, its population size continues to impact the Canadian electoral system.

 It is perhaps ironic that Alberta, for example, is more in tune with Quebec's concerns than Ontario. Political alienation breeds common interests. Both Alberta and Quebec have been fierce defenders of provincial jurisdiction. From the Constitution, natural resources, the securities industry, and a myriad of other issues affecting provincial matters, both have been onside. Ontario has never quite figured out how to debate and stand up to its own interests. Perhaps this is a result of the effect of being in the province with the national capital. Federal interests and the interests of Queen's Park may seem similar or even identical, even though this is clearly not the case when any federal government has to make an attempt to think and act nationally. Ontario has finally figured this out and is fighting fiercely for what it thinks is its share of fiscal transfers from Ottawa.

The situation in the Maritimes remains static. Promises of new shipbuilding are for the future. Pipelines running east from Alberta will work well for Maritimers in moving gas and oil into the area, preventing them from having to rely on middle-east oil. Newfoundland has found its way. Offshore oil has secured its future, and its renewable sources of hydro power for export are forever a source of income. Its problem is its relationship with Quebec. The power lines will be run under water to Nova Scotia, rather than through Quebec. There is no lost love between these two provinces as Quebec does not recognize Labrador as part of Newfoundland. The intergovernmental situation is sour, and seems incapable of being resolved.

The intergovernmental situation within Canada is not good. Quebec is not part of the Constitution and expresses its will in many ways. The West is thinking about a common identity, but provincial politics intervenes. Ontario is trying to define itself as something other than the centre of Canada, and as an equalization receiving province. The Maritimes struggle on, while Newfoundland moves forward with its newly acquired wealth in resources. The situation *en toto* is not good for a one Canada.

It is no longer good enough for Canadians to define themselves by what they are not: Americans; or by their health care system (many OECD countries have better ones); or by any myriad of symbols such as the game of hockey, the beaver, or the maple leaf. Without a national, pan-Canadian, vision of ourselves, we have little in the way of moving forward as one collective people.

Chapter 7
Federal-Provincial Fiscal Transfer Relations

1. Introduction

Any federal system of government requires a significant amount of cooperation between the orders of government to function satisfactorily. There is no more important extant area between the federal government and the provinces than fiscal transfers. This chapter addresses direct federal fiscal transfers from the federal government to the provinces; direct transfers of monies to individuals is not the subject here, though it is certainly relevant to the absolute personal needs and security of Canadians. The current federal-provincial-territorial fiscal transfer system is haphazard, uncooperative, and destined to create continuing strife among the jurisdictions. In US phraseology, it is on a cliff, a very wobbly one.

    The major transfers are the following: The Canada Health Transfer (CHT), Canada Social Transfer (CST) and the Equalization Program. Other transfers, such as Labour Market Training etc., should be noted, but are insignificant in terms of dollars relative to the aforementioned programs. The need for such transfers has always been obvious: provinces lack the fiscal means to carry out the constitutional responsibilities for their citizens in provinces' critical jurisdictional fields, mainly health care, education, and social services.

Metamorphosis is normally a term limited to the scientific world of insects, animals, and plants. The changing of one thing into another is always a marvel: cocoon to butterfly, polliwog to frog, seed to sunflower. There is a certain order to such changes, and evolution usually works very slowly, except maybe for bacteria and viruses.

Such is not the case with fiscal transfers in Canada. Changes have often been made willy-nilly and without the consent, and sometimes even consultation, of the provinces. They are conditioned by a centralist logic in Ottawa based on personalities and financial coffers, but always motivated by the political arena and ultimately re-election. Winning, after all, is the ultimate raison d'être of any political party.

The fiscal transfer system in Canada for health, post-secondary education and social services has no long term stability or evolution to it. It has morphed from a cost-shared system in the mid-fifties (a dollar raised=a dollar received) to a block-funded system in 1976-77 (no conditions on transfers for Health and Post-secondary education) - Established Programs Financing (EPF) and the Canada Assistance Plan (CAP), to a cap on CAP, to the more recent Canada Health Transfer (CHT) and Canada Social Transfer, a block-fund which under Prime Minister Martin at least guaranteed stable six percent yearly increases in funding for ten years ending in 2014.

With absolutely no negotiations with provinces and only superficial consultations, the federal government, under Prime Minister Harper, has limited growth in the CHT from 2016 to nominal GDP growth (economic growth, including inflation). Growth in this transfer could be as low as 2% yearly even though health care expenditures continue to advance at least 6% in most provinces.

The separate Equalization Program, now ensconced in the Constitution Act 1982, provides no conditions on funding for those provinces deemed unable to provide comparable services to their citizens at comparable rates of taxation. It is a straight transfer from the Consolidated Revenue Fund of the federal government to eligible provinces. The program started in 1957 and has always been geared to what the federal government Finance Department thought the government could afford, rather than the needs of the receiving provinces. In other words, Equalization formulae have always been based on an exercise in fiscal manipulation.

Quebec has persistently had a dominant impact on negotiations as it always receives well over half of national Equalization payments due to population, even though on a per capita basis Quebec receives much less than a province such as Prince Edward Island. The latest version of the program has reduced the sources of revenue to five, includes all provinces, and determines amounts given according to the original national average standard. The program has always been about jigging the revenue amount available to satisfy federal budgetary decisions. Courchene unabashedly states, "...equalization has resumed its unenviable state as an accident waiting to happen."[1] But it has been no accident. It has been about the failure of successive federal governments, Liberal and Conservative to engage in serious negotiations with provincial governments about fiscal capacities and consequent needs.

2. **Vertical Imbalances**

The following chart shows the distribution of federal transfers to provinces and territories for the fiscal years 2011-2014 as adapted from the Department of Federal Finance:[2]

$Billions(rounded)	2011-2012	2012-2013	2013-2014
Canada Health Transfer(CHT)	$26.9	$28.5	$30.3
Canada Social Transfer(CST)	$11.5	$11.8	$12.2
Equalization	$14.6	$15.4	$16.1
Territorial Financing	$2.8	$3.1	$3.3

The amounts transferred seem staggering (around $62 billion for 2013-2014), but, put in the context of own source provincial revenues garnered and spending required, the sums are paltry.

After all, the marquis financing deal in 1976-1977 under Established Programs Financing entailed 50-50 spending for health and post-secondary education. As well, the Canada Assistance Plan paid dollar for dollar funding of social services. There was a sense of stability in the transfer system and provinces did well by it, until the federal government made systematic financing changes beginning in 1982, which always ended in reduced growth, and sometimes year over year reductions in payments to the provinces. Reduced fiscal transfers were occurring at the same time as national health care expenditures were accelerating by double digits yearly.

Perhaps 1995 marked the nadir year in relations between the federal government and the provinces with respect to fiscal transfers. As part of the process of addressing its own growing budget deficits, Ottawa unilaterally reduced transfers significantly. This, of course, resulted in instability in provincial financial expectations, making their budgetary decisions trying. Transfers were cut in excess of $5.7 billion from 1996-1998[3] and, as Courchene has noted, this was more an exercise in the "federal savings power" than anything else.[4]

In a May 2005 media backgrounder, the Council of the Federation described the fiscal imbalance between the two orders of government this way: "... Vertical fiscal imbalance refers to a gap between revenue sources and spending responsibilities... it means one order of government collects more tax dollars than it needs... crowding out the ability of the other order of government to raise the revenue it needs to fund its responsibilities."[5]

Acrimonious federal-provincial fiscal relations, a series of unilateral changes since 1982, and a total mismatch of constitutional responsibilities versus fiscal capacity to carry out those responsibilities have all played a part in effecting a very discordant confederation in Canada. In an apparently futile attempt to address these serious issues in 2006, an Advisory Panel on Fiscal Imbalance produced a report to the

Council of the Federation (Premiers and Territorial Leaders) entitled, *Reconciling the Irreconcilable*.[6] The title itself is foreboding and suggests an oxymoronic outcome. Indeed, nothing has been reconciled, and the Harper government refuses to meet with Premiers to discuss this central issue of confederation, even as he made time in early 2013 to meet First Nations leaders for an entire day. As the following table demonstrates, federal fiscal transfers are only a small portion of total provincial revenues in most provinces:

Federal-Provincial Transfer Data

Provinces (All numbers rounded)	Federal Transfers ($B) (2011-2012) 1.	Revenue ($B) 2.	Transfers As % of Revenues	GDP By province ($B) 3.
BC	5.3	42	13	217
Alberta	3.4	39	9	296
Saskatchewan	1.2	11	11	75
Manitoba	3.4	14	24	56
Ontario	17.4	110	16	655
Quebec	17.2	65.5	26	346
Nova Scotia	2.6	8.6	30	37
New Brunswick	2.5	8	31	32
Prince Edward Island	.5	1.5	33	5.3
Newfoundland	1.1	8.3	13	34

1. *Federal Support to Provinces and Territories, Dept. of Finance 30/10/12*

2. *Data provided by Public Accounts each province and assembled by Dept. of Finance(2012)*

3. *Stats. Canada, CANSIM Table 384-0038(2011)*

Provinces (All numbers rounded)	Transfers as % of GDP	Federal Transfers as % total CHT, CST, Equalization Payments ($54.9 Billion) (2011-12)	Population by Province (M)(2012) 4.	Transfers per capita ($)
BC	2	10	4.62	872
Alberta	1	6	3.9	872
Saskatchewan	2	2	1.08	1111
Manitoba	6	6	1.27	2677
Ontario	3	32	13.5	1289
Quebec	5	31	8.05	2137
Nova Scotia	7	5	.949	2740
New Brunswick	8	5	.756	3309
Prince Edward Island	9	1	.146	3427
Newfoundland	3	2	.513	2144

4. *Stats. Canada, CANSIM Table 051-0001 (2012)*

At the low end, transfers only represent 9% of Alberta's revenues; at the high end, they represent a significant 33% of PEI's revenues. Clearly, a wealthy province like Alberta does not receive nearly its percentage share of transfers. This may change if oil and natural gas prices stay low. It's as if some provinces get a whole cake and some get a cupcake!

Another indicator of reliance is the relationship of federal transfers to GDP. Alarmingly, in five provinces, transfers amount to a negligible 1% to 3% of GDP The column on Federal Transfers as a percentage of total transfers is indicative of the disparities among the provinces. Ontario and Quebec garner 63% of transfers, close to their percentage of population, while British Columbia and Alberta account for only 16% even though their share of total population is 24.3%, 50% less than their share of population.

The final column reveals Transfers per capita ($). In 2011-2012, British Columbia and Alberta received $872 per capita, while the average per capita transfer was $2058. Clearly, most of the difference in federal transfer shares is due to the Equalization Program, although Alberta has always been shortchanged in CHT. CST calculations as one time tax points (the EPF tax transfer in 1977) are calculated prior to the cash component. This irritation finally gets rectified in 2014.

There is indeed a dramatic fiscal imbalance, given that provinces and territories are responsible for funding the most important spending fields of health, education and social services. As an example, Alberta spent about $16.6 billion on health care in 2012-13 but only received $2.3 billion in federal fiscal transfers or about 14% for this program area. Under the original Established Programs Financing Agreement 1976-1977 the province received roughly 50%. This dramatic decline in federal financing is yet another indicator of dysfunction in the federation; there can be no "reconciling the irreconcilable" without a fundamental reordering of the taxpayer system.

This historical offloading of the federal deficit onto the provinces since 1982 has, of course, resulted in increased provincial deficits and debt in most provinces. Cooperative fiscal federalism disappeared in that year. Animus could well have been expected with unilateral federal decision-making and "going through the motions" style non-negotiations.

In the report to the Council of the Federation cited above, provinces cited the following concerns about the state of fiscal federalism:

1. The realities of provincial expenditure pressures and inadequacy of financial arrangements to meet provincial needs.

2. The unwarranted use of the federal spending power in areas of exclusive provincial jurisdiction, disregarding provincial priorities and placing additional financial pressures on provincial governments.

3. They deplored the lack of mechanisms for dialogue and the ad hoc nature of intergovernmental relationships and arrangements.[7]

The second point has already been addressed in the chapter on the spending power. The first point is clearly relevant to this chapter and it has been shown that the federal government has abandoned its original commitments due to its own perceived financial pressures, needs and responsibilities.

There is no doubt that the federal government is responsible for some key areas, including foreign affairs and defense, the treasury , critical direct transfers to citizens, including OAS, GIS etc. And addressing federal debt issues is a persistent concern. However, it needs to be pointed out that the Harper government's decision to reduce the GST to 5% from 7% costs its consolidated revenue fund about $14 billion yearly. Even if half of those monies had been plowed back in fiscal transfers, it would have gone far in reducing the pressures on provincial constitutional responsibilities, particularly health care and education.

3. Redressing the Imbalance

Nonetheless, provinces' expenditure responsibilities for health, education, social services, seniors, infrastructure, municipalities and so on far outstrip the federal government's own responsibilities. Federal-provincial fiscal relations are only likely to become more disharmonious without substantive changes regarding the transferring of adequate taxpayer dollars commensurate with provincial responsibilities.

There are only a few means to realize such a transfer:

1. Cost-sharing arrangements (a dollar spent in a province results in an additional dollar received)

2. Block-fund (as per the CHT and CST arrangements where there are few or no conditions)

3. Tax transfer (where the federal government cedes tax room to the provinces and the provinces swallow up this room so that the taxpayer is left in virtually the same situation as before, except more goes to provinces). As an illustrative example, dropping the Goods and Services Tax rate to 5% from 7% left open room for some provinces to occupy that room and increase their provincial sales taxes.

The only scenario which results in a permanent transfer over which future federal governments would have no control is the last one. Is it likely that a federal government would transfer tax room again? No. The major transfer of tax room (13.5% personal income tax points and 1% corporate tax room) as part of the 1976-77 Fiscal Arrangements is very unlikely to recur. Even though the provinces simply received back a portion of what they gave up to the federal government during WWII, the federal government's own financial requirements and recession cycles have partially dictated its federal-provincial fiscal transfer decisions.

Moreover, and much more importantly, transfers of tax room would loosen the power of the federal government to direct provincial spending decisions. Tax transfers automatically equate to less control and the federal government understands this well. By definition, any federal government perceives itself as an overseer of the federation. This means central direction and nationally imposed programs.

But the obstinacy of holding on to extra tax room even though the provinces constitutional responsibilities clearly require such room are stressing the federation to the point of fiscal transfer meltdown. This vertical imbalance is unsustainable.

4. Horizontal Imbalances

Another central part of the problem of fiscal transfers is that there is a horizontal fiscal imbalance in the Canadian federation as expressed in the analysis of the above chart. A horizontal imbalance, unlike the artificial vertical one, is endemic to any federation where wealth is distributed totally disproportionately according to the available revenue sources of each unit. These include personal income taxes, corporate taxes, sales taxes, natural resource revenues and a myriad of other sources, including lottery revenue, tobacco taxes, gas taxes, etc.

The Equalization Program is the principal means of rectifying such balances but the program, as noted, is ad hoc and subject to the whims of the Department of Finance. Other means of rectifying the imbalance, while appropriate or not, include disparate Employment Insurance requirements from province to province and various programs to address regional disparities, which, after all, is also included in the Constitution Act, 1982.

Currently, all provinces except BC, Alberta, Saskatchewan and Newfoundland receive equalization payments. Alberta has not received payments since the mid-60s and Newfoundland is a recent addition to the "have" club due to its offshore oil. Ontario is a recent addition to the "have not" club, even with its over-powering manufacturing base relative to all other provinces. Saskatchewan has drifted in and out of equalization entitlements, but its natural resource base would seem to ensure its non-receiving status.

Issues arise both between equalization receiving provinces versus non-receiving provinces, as well as among the receiving provinces themselves. As to the first situation, Alberta, and now BC and Saskatchewan, are arguing that its taxpayers are indirectly over-equalizing to the receiving provinces. It is important to note that the Equalization Program is solely a federal program; monies are transferred directly from its Consolidated Revenue Fund to the eligible provinces. Transfers are absolutely not from the treasuries of have provinces to have not provinces.

The argument that over-equalization prevails is that some of the receiving provinces have, as an example, more doctors, nurses and teachers per capita than the "donor" provinces. Alberta has never pressed this issue very far when the equalization program is up for re-negotiation for obvious reasons: No province wants to appear to be greedy, particularly Alberta, which for many, many years has had a fiscal capacity per capita far in excess of any other province. Nonetheless, doubts are now being raised about the amounts of equalization being divvied out yearly. Alberta has generally taken the high road. However this is a systemic source of dysfunction and is likely to be exacerbated now that Ontario qualifies and receives substantial payments.

The Constitution Act, 1982 entrenches equalization payments. The problem is that what is in the Act bears no causal relationship to what is paid out. The key condition in the act, providing "reasonably comparable services at reasonably comparable rates of taxation", is nebulous. What counts as reasonably comparable services? All provinces are different in terms of their requirements and needs. If Quebec decides to have a Cadillac day care system and Alberta opts to provide significantly more benefits to its senior citizens, does that then mean that ALL provinces should be provided with the financial means to support such programs? Should equalization be used to fund extra programs, such as Quebec's? Is there any way to establish criteria to match comparable services with comparable rates of taxation?

The equalization gnomes in Ottawa may very well be able to compute or manipulate the meaning of comparable rates of taxation at the front end, but are severely ill-equipped to determine comparable services at the delivery end. Those decisions are made in the provinces based on citizen's needs and their own political agendas.

There are also issues among the receiving provinces. There is a general feeling that Ontario should not be entitled to Equalization because its per capita personal income tax is higher than other receiving provinces (Ontario was eliminated before when just such a proviso was placed into the formula). Various transition arrangements for Newfoundland and Labrador and Nova Scotia have strained relations with some other receiving provinces. It is a fixed pot and if more goes here than there, then some are going to get less. Saskatchewan has certainly made arguments that it has been adversely affected through such arbitrary changes. Haggling over limited federal dollars for equalization payments may work delightfully to the benefit of the federal government; divide and conquer is stone-age power politics and economics. But it does little to keep the federation together.

The fiscal transfer cliff in Canada has nothing to do with a lack of federal revenues. It is a system that is broken because the provinces lack the fiscal capacity to carry out their critical constitutional responsibilities in the major spending areas of health, education, and social services, which are over 80% of total expenditures in some provinces. That the federal government is prepared to go over the cliff to satisfy and satiate its own obfuscated agenda is telling. Canadians are slowly, but surely, losing their most cherished social programs and they may not always understand why. As the Caledon Institute put it recently, "Canada is no longer a practicing fiscal union, at least in respect of using fiscal federalism to mitigate fiscal imbalance."[8]

There is one other way to look at inflows and outflows. This is essentially what flows out of each province and what comes back to it in terms of fiscal transfers etc. The following table, adapted from Mansell and Schlenker, illustrates the point perfectly:

Total and per capita fiscal balances (1961-1992)

Province	Balances(1994 dollars, billions)	Per capita
BC	-6.1	-11
Alberta	139	2096
Saskatchewan	-36	-1.2
Manitoba	-50	-1.5
Ontario	45	183
Quebec	-168	-803
New Brunswick	-63	-2.9
Nova Scotia	-95	-3.5
Prince Edward Island	-15	-3.9
Newfoundland	-56	-3.2

(Adapted from Robert Mansell and Ronald Schlenker, The Provincial Distribution of Federal Fiscal Balances, Canadian Business Economics, Winter 1995, p. 6)

Their work is eye-popping, brilliant, and has never been contested. While the data is dated, it indicates the extent of the imbalances in this federation. Between 1961 and 1992, Alberta has been a net contributor of $139 billion while Quebec has been a net receiver of $168 billion. Only Alberta and Ontario have been net contributors to the federation during this period. No doubt, the NEP period added to these numbers substantially, but the fact remains that Alberta is the big revenue weight lifter within Canada and this is causing rifts within the nation. The continuing net contributions from the big "giver" provinces does not auger well for the federation if, indeed, economics is a large determiner of political futures.

Since Ontario is the main supplier for "have not" provinces, it is a significant net gainer from such exports. Alberta does not have the manufacturing capability to produce the good to gain such benefits, and so its net contribution may indeed have exceeded $200 billion.

Alberta's outflow contribution to confederation does not go unnoticed within the province.

5. Conclusions

Harold Lasswell's 1936 US Political Science classic, *Who Gets What, When, How* is as appropriate today as ever.[9] Politics, indeed, is largely about the distribution of economic goods and power. Canada is no exception to this concept, even if it seems self-serving and greedy. Perhaps Carousel Eight only applies to individual good deeds after all. Fiscal transfers are about distributions of cash to provinces.

> The problems with Canada's fiscal transfer system are numerous:
> 1. There is no **transparency** to the system as only a small cohort of federal and provincial finance officials have a real understanding of it, particularly the Equalization Program.
> 2. There is no **accountability** to the public, largely due to the first point.
> 3. There are no **negotiations**. A full negotiations process, resulting in the typical five year agreement, has been replaced with a partial consultative process.
> 4. There are **Vertical inequities,** the unwillingness of the federal government to address the fiscal imbalance between its revenues and provincial constitutional responsibilities.
> 5. There are **Horizontal issues, i.e.** who is over and under compensated.

That none of these issues is being addressed at all does not bode well for the future of Canada. After all, economic matters do have a long reach within this country.

Chapter 8
Canadian Foreign Policy

1. Introduction

Canadian foreign policy is in a state of disarray. In seven years, the Harper government has managing to overturn fifty years of the carefully orchestrated policies of both Liberal and Conservative governments in the delicate political and economic international environment. A succinctly nourished middle-power diplomatic mandate encouraging peaceful resolutions to conflict, full involvement in multilateral activities, contributing reasonable amounts of foreign aid, and promulgating fair foreign trade is being abruptly reversed. A basic and profound re-positioning of Canada's role in the world is being undertaken. This is yet another timely example of how this country's raison d'être is unravelling before our eyes.

Sometimes a country is identified partly by how other countries perceive it; sometimes it is identified as well by how it perceives itself in the international milieu. Canada is a prime example of both. Certainly, since the Second World War, this country has been seen externally as a full participant in a number of organizational alliances such at NATO and NORAD. It has also been involved in an extensive list of multinational entities, and integrally involved in any number of governmental agencies: the OECD, G-8, and G-20 on the economic front; environmental issues; and NGOs, with planned parenthood as an example.

At the same time, it has been relied on, and understood to be, a coordinating power in addressing and resolving key issues such as the Suez Crisis in 1956. And it has been perhaps the world's most willing participant in peacekeeping operations in a number of countries, including Cyprus, Yemen, and Congo. As a middle-power, Canada has been perceived as a key contributor to UN diplomatic activities that could lead to peaceful resolutions of conflict. In the past, Canada has been greatly admired for its efforts. The image of how Canada has been perceived by others externally has been seen and honoured internally by Canadians as well. A palpable pride has been exuded by the citizenry since the mid-1950s regarding how this country has finessed and wiggled its way into a bold, central, diplomatic role in the international environment in ways in which even the US, the former USSR, China, England, and France have been unable to match.

Viable diplomacy, support for international development initiatives, environmental quality, support for a number of human rights conventions such as the UN Convention on the Rights of the Child, removal of land mines, and fairer trade are all marking points of the Canadian middle power strategy. It may be partly a self-serving "feel good" diplomacy but it has, nonetheless, become an integral part of how Canadians see themselves in the broader international environment. It is part of the ethos of a historical, palpable and tangible Canadian identity.

A state's self-identity is undoubtedly always based on partial myths about its role in the international system. Canada is no exception, yet this country has been able to occupy pivotal roles which have, on occasion, been the envy of the most powerful states. As previously mentioned, Canada's role in resolving the Suez Crisis in 1956 is an important example. Its peace-keeping role in Cyprus, keeping the Greek and Turkish Cypriots from warring with one another, which could have caused a major international crisis had Greece and Turkey taken up arms against each other, is another. Financial aid sent through the Canadian International Development Agency to many third world countries, including a nascent, boycott-free, democratic South Africa, has increased Canada's respected position in the international system.

2. Soft Power

It has done this with soft power. This term is Joseph Nye's important narrative of how best to influence others to coincide their foreign policies with yours without resorting to coercion.[1] This may be a modern version of attracting more flies with honey than vinegar. Soft power implicitly rejects conflict and war as "tool box" possibilities, and emphasizes the need for diplomacy and continued foreign aid as instruments of conflict resolution. It rejects Clausewitz's factual assessment in *On War* that war is simply diplomacy by other means.[2] Perhaps soft power is naïve, but it offers alternative possibilities to hostile aggression and trade sanctions as central mechanisms in resolving conflicts among nations.

For the most part, Canada would fit since the mid-nineteen fifties into the more dovish, rather than hawkish, category as a middle-power. Part of this is about Canada's ideological perspective toward the international political environment. Generally, a universal, catholic perception has governed a narrow-minded myopic one. Even during the heights of the Great Cold War, Canada did not always take sides: pro NATO versus pro Warsaw Pact; pro domino effect in Asia vis-à-vis a more cosmopolitan approach. While firmly committed to the UN actions against North Korea in that war, Canada was non-supportive of the Vietnam War and, indeed, welcomed likewise minded American youth to find a home in this country whether they were undrafted, drafted, or deserting. It can never be easy to take on the great "elephant" on the border, but there is a begrudging respect about Canada's self-willed manner in the highest places in Washington, DC.

Another example includes the unwillingness of this country to place any sanctions on Cuba and, in fact, to encourage travel to that country as well as being supportive of a number of successful business operations. This has surely been a sore point in bilateral US-Canada relations, particularly among the politically motivated Cuban expatriates that have migrated mainly to Florida. They carry disproportionate political weight and incessantly pressure both Democrats and Republicans to heed their call. US foreign policy is quite clearly motivated as much by domestic electoral issues as anything else. There are other examples: Prime Minister Diefenbaker's obstinance toward placing US nuclear missiles on Canadian soil; Prime Minister Mulroney's antipathy toward President Reagan and British Prime Minister Thatcher with regard to their opposition to the boycott against the racist South African regime; and, most recently, Prime Minister Chretien's, Martin's and Harper's refusal to support direct military involvement in President Bush's abject, propagandistic "coalition of the willing" in Iraq.

In all cases, the positions that Canada has taken have proven to be historically correct and have certainly garnered support throughout the world in both developed and developing third world nations. US involvement, with close to half a million soldiers at one point in the Vietnam War, proved to be an absolute disaster and very nearly threw that country into revolution: turning mother against father and father against son and some areas of the nation against others. As for Iraq, no weapons of mass destruction were ever found, thereby totally obliterating any reasoning for intervention there. Conversely, Nelson Mandela's rapprochement with the white community in South Africa is a testament to what can happen with soft power, and certainly the boycott sanctions against the previous regimes by Canada and most of the rest of the world played a central role.

A balanced approach to the international global system has paid off in dividends such as support for Canada to be selected on six occasions as a temporary member of the prestigious UN Security Council. Admittedly, such membership is more symbolic than anything else, as the five permanent members can exercise powerful veto power, which the temporary members cannot, but it still carries some weight in the international community.

Travelling Americans often wear Canadian flags on their lapels in such places as France to obtain better service and acceptance. Canadians do likewise so as not to be confused with Americans. The non-ideological approach has worked well in Canada's international relations as well as in individual interpersonal and travel activities.

3. Hard Power

Back in the mid-nineties, Jim Dinning, Minister of Finance with the Alberta Government, coined the phrase, "Normal doesn't live in Alberta anymore."[3] This was in reference to Alberta's misguided actions to justify draconian cuts in its budget to address deficit and debt issues. It was a rallying call to treat government budgets as if they were family budgets. How is this relevant to Canada's foreign policy decisions today? It is pertinent because it articulates a new hard line in Canadian foreign policy that is a signature departure from the soft power diplomatic strategies of the past.

Some of this evolution started in the 1990's with Canada's move from peace-keeping (Cyprus) to peace-making under NATO (Bosnia, Croatia). Peace-making is more warlike in comparison, where the UN's role is to keep opposing parties from fighting. Peace-making takes sides and usually involves some form of combat. A more recent example would be Canada's role through NATO in Libya.

As Canada is a middle-power, the meaning of hard power here is quite different than it is for a major super power such as the US, which continues to be the world's preeminent, dominant power in both the world economy as well as militarily. Hard power in Canada represents a perceptive shift, particularly since 2006, to place emphasis on coercion rather than peace-keeping and to emphasize blatant commercial self-interests over humanitarian ones. The most dramatic example is Canada's continuing involvement in military activities in Afghanistan. The mission has never been clear, and militaries do not work well without concrete objectives.

There is little doubt that Canadian activity there is a quid pro quo to the Americans for Canada's unwillingness to participate militarily in Iraq. In all fairness, given the overwhelming leverage that the US has over this country in trade matters, there may have been little room for Canada to maneuver. After all, 75%, or thereabouts, of exports are destined for the US. Trade dependency limits what can be done in US-Canada relations.

Canadian hard power was perhaps best articulated on November 27, 2013, by Ed Fast, Minister of International Trade: "We must be more aggressive and effective than the intense competition we face as we advance Canada's commercial interests in key global markets. This new plan represents a sea change in the way Canada's diplomatic assets are deployed around the world…".[4] Future "diplomatic" efforts are to focus on the needs of business rather than those of citizens and traditional diplomacy. In adapting to a fiercely competitive international trade environment, government emphasis is now to be trained on business needs. Particular attention is to be placed on small and medium sized business enterprises (SMES). This is all part of the Global Markets Action Plan, first enunciated in 2006.

This part of hard power entrenches "economic diplomacy" as the new mantra of Canadian diplomacy.[5] Diplomacy is to be turned into a business, and no longer Bismarck's "art of the possible." For Canada, the art of the possible was perhaps most entrenched during Prime Minister Pearson's leadership: full participation in UN agencies, NATO, Non-governmental organization (NGO) support, foreign aid .and, of course, trade enhancement. It is a mix of realpolitik and idealism. This evolving middle-power strategy worked well for Canada for over half a century.

A pseudo crass emphasis on Canadian diplomats playing handmaidens to businesses to increase their trade prospects and profits internationally is anathema to anything vaguely related to the past in Canadian foreign policy circles. It is indeed a sea change, and Canada's fine diplomatic entourage must be greatly discouraged. Surely, diplomacy cannot be about just pure greed.

Of course, the international economic environment is competitive, and one in five Canadian jobs is dependent on exports and imports. Nonetheless, the far reach of diplomacy extends to compassion for so many of the countries of the world that are so much less fortunate than Canadians. It is about finding resolutions to conflict rather than seeking military solutions. It is about helping Canadians in foreign lands find their way if passports are lost, etc. "Economic diplomacy" has xenophobic overtones; Canada is being labelled in some domestic and international circles as an international renegade. How shocking is that?

4. Diplomacy Lost

The following table attempts to show the differences in how diplomacy used to be exercised in this country in contradistinction to the new, upstart diplomacy. The categories should be seen only as a heuristic device or learning tool and may overemphasize certain aspects of the changes that are being implemented in Canada's foreign relations.

Canadian Foreign Policy Table

1955 - 2006	Harper 2006 - onward
(Soft Power)	(Hard Power)
Multilateralism (involvement)	Unilateralism (isolation)
Engagement	Disengagement
Peace-Keeping	Peace-Making
Diplomacy and Trade	The Business of Trade
US/World Focus	Drifting Focus
Gradual Change Through Continuity	Radical Policy Shift

Foreign Affairs Minister Baird went before the U.N on September 30, 2013, and said the following: "Canada's government doesn't seek to have our values... validated by elites who would rather go along to get along."[6] Which elites is he alluding to, and whoever said that Canada should go along to get along? It looks a lot like striking out at false straw men. Is the tsunami "sea change" in foreign policy directed at upsetting the professional foreign policy service which the Canadian regime sees as entrenched, or is it aimed at the whole structure of UN? Or both? In some respects, it seems almost as conspiratorial and paranoid as the mainly defunct far right wing John Birch Society's views on the need for the US to withdraw from the UN altogether!

What the Harper government no longer wants to "go along" with is the very notion of multilateralism. This can be broadly defined this way: First, seeking accommodations among like-minded nation-states to resolve major conflicting views, crises, and situations; and, second, to promote broad trade agreements intended to be for the benefit of the respective participants. At its core, multilateralism entails compromise and accommodation and tolerance for perspectives which may not be easily subsumed under one's own national banner.

The masses of Canadian tourists heading to Cuba in the winter in no way means that Canadians (the government or citizens) accept all of the policies of the Cuban government, including human rights abuses. "Going along" and "Getting along" has offered Canadians opportunities to understand cultures and ideas which Americans, for example, cannot fathom because there is hardly any exposure to them. And it has served Canadians well in broadening their perspectives, while enriching the lives of individuals in those countries where they visit.

Unilateralism is the opposite of multilateralism. It means a state is acting on its own without any attempt to seek other states' support. It can be implemented based on some ideological sense of moral purpose or internal paranoia, for example North Korea, or it can be ignited and encouraged by self-serving electoral politics based on domestic concerns. It has been a common nation-state strategy to seek out foreign enemies as a means to unify itself internally. This worked well for

Germany before WWII and for the US, for that matter, during the Cold War.

In the case of Canada, a more benign yet crass example may include attempts to secure future electoral support in select ethnic ridings within Canada. Canada's zealous defense of anything Israel does would certainly garner support in key Montreal and Toronto ridings. Prime Minister Harper's snubbing of the 2013 Commonwealth Conference for fear of alienating Sri Lankan refugees domiciled in Toronto ridings is another example. His unwillingness to address the UN in both 2012 and 2013 for ideological reasons, while sending Ministers instead, is certainly insulting to that organization and affirms a growing Canadian isolation from multilateral venues.

Unilateralism disengages Canada from the broad world community of about 200 nations. It is befuddling that this country has turned this way in just the past seven years, and certainly must be confounding to foreign governments. Canada's isolation is not in the same category as North Korea, Iran, Burma, Cambodia, or maybe Cuba, since none of these countries makes any pretense to be bastions of democracy. Their sole motive for isolation is to maintain power over their peoples and, besides the blatant use of intimidation and military force, the best way to do this is to circle the wagons and close off citizens' access to international media and direct foreign contact. As one of the universally recognized foremost democracies, Canada's isolation is obviously significantly different.

It may have some of its roots that go back to Cold War thinking and its aftermath. Personalities and parties are informed through their respective histories. There can be little doubt that the foreign policy perspectives of the Harper machine have been conditioned by the Reform Party, predecessor to the existing Conservative Party. Taking the "Progressive" out of the Conservative Party should have been fair grist for those that comment on political parties that a radical shift in domestic and foreign policies might transpire if and when that party gained a majority government. It would be a move to the right.

Alberta Conservatives are very much influenced by their American counterparts and, in particular, the influx of Texans, Oklahomans, Kansans and everywhere else where people make their lives from oil and gas. Those values, in addition to the traditional farming values, even though worth only three percent of Alberta's GDP, have come to permeate the ideological perspectives of Albertans generally. Intergenerational political perspectives in this province evolve slowly, if at all. It explains why Alberta has voted Conservative ever since 1970, and explains why the major challenge to the government was the Wild Rose Party which leans even much further to the right.

After migrating from Ontario, Harper eventually fully embraced the Alberta ideological perspective. In international politics, this would mean support of key American positions: punishing enemies and rewarding friends; isolating Iraq, Iran, and North Korea; absolute support for Israel, even as they would continue to build settlements on Palestinian lands and fail to recognize it as a state. It would go further to include, as does US foreign policy, a deep suspicion of UN Conventions and the general worth of that organization as means of conflict resolution and economic development. The Alberta homeland is a major source for the positions taken in Canadian foreign policy today. At least in foreign policy, it seems that the Canadian West has overtaken traditional Ottawa multilateral diplomacy in favour of a more American insular type of diplomacy. The problem with emulating the American approach is that Canada is not a super power in any way, whereas the US is in all ways. Canada is a middle power, even if it is part of the G-8. It has not roamed the hallways of the Pentagon lobbying to obtain a Trident nuclear submarine, for example, which would put it in a superpower category shared only with the US.

For over a century, US foreign policy has had an almost Messianic mission in "making the world safe for democracy," and ensuring that the first mission facilitates and augments American corporate interests throughout the world nation-state system. If this means toppling democratically elected regimes, such as President Allende in Chile, or support for autocratic regimes throughout Central and South America, the Middle-East, or other places in the world, so be it. This is raw, hard power; it is definitely neo-imperial. And it is not Canada.

In terms of insularity, the US regularly fails to support UN Conventions. It would not even support the UN Convention on the Rights of the Child, aimed principally at ridding the world of child slavery and prostitution. It is even opposed to the elimination of landmines. One never knows where enemies may be in the future and what measures may be required to thwart them. Such views are anathema to the perspectives of most nations, including Canada, which has been a world leader on eliminating land mines, for example.

Hard power as an instrument of diplomacy is not available to Canada militarily. Building an ice-breaker or two to defend debatable claims the country is making about the North Pole and the arctic is indefensible and probably laughable. Only through soft power will the involved parties resolve passage access issues due to global warming and future development, if any, in the Arctic.

The hard power aspect of Canada's shifted, disengaging, diplomacy is also based upon a concerted effort to eschew international mechanisms to address and resolve critical issues related to global warming. Canada was a key contributor to the Kyoto Accord, which required nations to reduce CO_2 emissions to below 1990 levels. The protocol was signed in 1998 and ratified in 2002. It was announced in December 2011 that Canada was withdrawing from the Protocol. Environmental Minister Kent said, "Kyoto for Canada is in the past. As such, we are invoking our legal right to formally withdraw."[7] One of the arguments is that Canada only contributes about 2% of emissions, but it would cost many billions to meet decreased targets. Another is that countries such as China, India etc. in the so-called developing world would not be required or be penalized to meet what would be, in theory, their reduction targets. But the real motivation for withdrawal is a self-interested one. Oil Sands companies in the Fort McMurray area are a major contributor to emission amounts, but certainly not the only ones (coal fired electricity companies, mining interests in Ontario, etc.). This narrow, myopic vision is costing Canada diplomatic goodwill and credit.

This underscores a severely misguided government focus on turning diplomacy into the business of trade. There is no effort to take a balanced approach emphasizing economic prosperity, an understanding of key economic evolutionary differences between so-called developed and developing countries and protection of the environment. Yet another example is Canada's 2013 abandonment of the UN Convention to Combat Desertification. Canada is the only country out of 195 to do this. What is the rationale? Is it a denial of what the overwhelming scientific community has been saying for decades about the consequences of global warming? The ostensible reason is that the money spent is going to bureaucracy rather than programming. Canada was only contributing $315 thousand a year to this Convention and it seems petty to withdraw unilaterally. "It is not an effective way to spend taxpayers' money," the Prime minister said.[8]

5. Canada/US Relations

No matter what government is in power in Canada, foreign policy will always centre on Canada/US trade relations. Two-way trade exceeded $680 billion ($US) in 2011. Canada is the second largest export market to the US; the US is the largest import market for Canada. The numbers are staggering, approaching $2 billion US per day, and are not nearly matched anywhere else in the world in terms of two-way trade. Given this amount of trade, it is no surprise that rectifying some issues is difficult if the interests are not identical or easily resolved. Such is the case with the following sample of issues: the Keystone pipeline, soft wood lumber exports, procurement policies, border security issues, building a new Detroit/Windsor Bridge to facilitate trade, agricultural subsidies and patent/intellectual protection. The US responds to most of these issues in light of its own domestic electoral politics. Keystone is certainly the most flagrant example as President Obama is playing politics with a significant part of his Democratic political base: the environmentalists. This is a mirror image of Prime Minister Harper's efforts to protect the dairy industry against cheap imports of milk, cheese and other dairy products from the US and Europe. The latter may be mitigated with the recently adopted Canada-E.U Agreement.

The problem with Canada is that it cannot mimic the US: this is indeed "Me and mini-me" as was so comically portrayed in *The Spy Who Shagged Me*.[9] Canada is a middle power. It has never made any pretenses to becoming anything else. The mighty elephant to the south influences and conditions the Canadian identity in many ways: trade, defense matters, political culture, media influences, size of markets and so forth. Based on these differences in power, it is obvious that any Canadian government would establish a sound lobbying base in Washington, D.C. to pursue its interests and they do. So do several provinces. Grabbing attention is the first step to obtaining good outcomes.

This is no reason, however, for Canada to play handmaiden to US spying systems in the National Security Agency. Apparently, the latest Ed Snowden revelations indicate that Canada has had its own spying systems (collecting information in nefarious ways) on other countries for over twenty years and has been supplying this information at the behest of the USWhere are the dividends of this castrated concept of sovereignty? Canada and Ontario have had to guarantee the building of the new Detroit Bridge; Keystone is still a pipe dream, so to speak. The US scoffs at Canadian claims to the Arctic. Softwood lumber exports never seem to get resolved permanently. Special labelling for meats exported to the US adds to the insults. There is little pay-off for Canada's efforts.

Oh, continued mini-me participation in NORAD? What jets are scrambled when the Russians get a bit too close to Alaska or Canadian territory: American ones out of Washington State? Why isn't the defense base at Comox on Vancouver Island up to snuff in defending the West? The lack of defense spending and preparation in Canada is appalling and has consequences, including erosion of political sovereignty. Reliance on a foreign country to provide one's own defense has never worked very successfully in the history of nations. And it always comes at a price. Pressing Canada to buy the latest US jet (F-35) at exorbitant prices and no firm schedule for delivery is another example. All of this is clearly not the result of the past eight years of the Harper regime, but it is certainly part of continuing with what does not work.

Canada has tried to broaden its trade agreements in the Americas, Europe, and China with limited results. The Harper government seems to prefer bilateral style agreements and, except for the US, this does not seem to materialize into substantive agreements and benefits for Canada. The trade mix seems to show that well into the future over 70% or more of Canadian trade will be with one trade partner: the US Such dependence is yet another example of a declining country in search of itself.

6. Conclusions

Canada has a proud historical tradition in foreign policy. As a middle power, it has always been about threading the needle in bilateral relations with the US. And it has never been easy. Sometimes it is a matter of the personality of the leaders or philosophical differences of the political parties in power in each country. US' hostile suspicions about anything in the international political environment that could slightly, conceivably affect in the slightest way their political sovereignty is always met with rejection. The US system of separation of powers has contributed to the malaise to the South as two-thirds agreement of the Senate is required to ratify treaties. Canada is not limited in this way, although the agreement of all provinces to international Conventions etc. limits what is possible here as well.

In the past fifty-plus years, Canada has been a full participant in UN activities. Peace-keeping has earned Canada much respect. This is not the business of making war, but preventing antagonists from internecine fighting and going to war in areas like Cyprus. Who would want Greece and Turkey to go to war? Canada's full engagement in UN organizations and in international conventions has served the country well and earned respect throughout the world. While commitments to foreign aid have fallen below promises, at least there has been an attempt to follow through by way of such organizations as the Canadian International Development Agency (CIDA). Canada's recent efforts in Haiti in the aftermath of that horrific earthquake have been exemplary. Humility, compassion and generosity have been an integral part of the Canadian ethos.

What has changed most dramatically over the past seven years in foreign policy is that a much more narrow self-interested focus has been the dominant theme over a more universalistic approach. The consequences have been dramatic. Portugal was chosen over Canada to be a temporary member of the National Security Council at the UN; the refusal of the Prime Minister to deliver speeches to the UN and to avoid participation at Commonwealth, Francophone, and the Organization of American States organizations undergirds a pattern of withdrawal from multilateral activities. Withdrawals from the Kyoto Protocol and the Desertification Convention augment the perception that Canada is withdrawing from international activities in a major way. The world of nations must be befuddled by such an amazing reversal of roles in the international environment. Canada can no longer be counted on.

A self-interested emphasis on bilateral deals in trade is unlikely to serve Canada well. A country's foreign policy interests are not limited to what the government can fetch for its corporations externally. Trade has always been a part of what foreign offices have attempted to contribute to but has never been the central defining characteristic. This is indeed a sea change in emphasis. Embassies are about helping citizens. They are about facilitating the activities of non-governmental organizations. They are about helping potential immigrants get the papers right and so on. A simplistic emphasis on one aspect of the foreign policy role on the business of business is greed-like and very un-Canadian.

Soft power emphasizes diplomatic means as the principal tool of conflict resolution and evolution within the international political system. Multilateralism is a key means to this end. Hard power exploits the economic and military weapons that a country can mobilize to have its way in the world. Canada is hardly placed as a middle power to exercise hard power, as most of its trade is quite dependent upon the US and it is a fumbling act in the military category. Yet it is hard power and unilateral actions that have become a defining characteristic of the Harper regime. It is no wonder that other nations and their citizens are shaking their heads about where Canada is going. More and more Canadians are wondering the same thing. This chapter is yet one more example of Canada in decline from international activities in a major way. Canada can no longer be counted on.

Chapter 9
Conclusions

There has been no attempt in this manuscript to identify or address any number of other serious problems that contribute to the general malaise of Canadian society. Such issues would certainly include, but not at all be limited to, the severe income inequalities that are tolerated or even embraced in this country; the impacts of the energy industry on global warming and the environment; treatment of First Nations Peoples and the lack of treaty resolution; the decline of health care and educational standards as related to any number of other nation-states in the world; or ameliorating pernicious trans-border issues with the US which often seem to be intractable.

Rather, the focus has been on the lack of a true Canadian identity, on the failure of Canada's political institutions federally, the abject unravelling of federal-provincial relations, compounded by intergovernmental tensions, and the severe self-interested downgrading of Canadian foreign policy as perceived both domestically and internationally. Any one of these matters would undermine the functioning of any modern nation-state. That Canada is experiencing all of them simultaneously does not bode well for a commodious future for this country.

There can be little doubt that its historical, political heritage has had a major impact upon what Canada would become as a country over time. Demographic history within this country has certainly defined its evolution politically. The French and English invasion would mold a two-nation political ideology which attempted to unite two different, distinct and possibly contradictory models into one. While both models share democratic philosophies, the individualistic British inheritance would certainly be somewhat disharmonious with the more collective, communitarian influence of the French. The contradiction was built into the nation from the very start.

No doubt, the massive influx migration of American Loyalists during and after the American Revolution in 1776 changed the teeter-totter political balance between the English and French peoples forever. While this diaspora would be paltry by today's refugee emigration standards in places like Syria and South Sudan, these numbers were enough to have a significant impact on the future of Canadian politics.

Framing the BNA Act, 1867, would never have been an easy task, but time was of the essence, given the US civil war and its aftermath. The US was definitely in an expansionary mindset and was heavily armed. There was no alternative but to cobble together what was doable at the time. Pasting together a unitary British type system together with a US style federal system would be a formidable endeavour. Is it even possible?

A unitary British type of system is based on responsible government. There is one representative government responsible for the entire union. The Prime Minister and Cabinet must keep the confidence of the House of Commons. A federal system is based on the federal principle. This entails a distribution of federal and provincial (state) powers delineated in a constitution where each order of government is supreme to exercise its powers.

Adding on to this is the two-nation concept of English and French, thereby guaranteeing language, educational and cultural rights to the latter. And finally, establishing a judiciary that would become quite independent of legislatures, federal and provincial, completes the unsustainable package. Trying to fit triangles into circles and stars into squares never quite works!

S.91(3) of the Constitution Act, 1982, clearly establishes the right of the federal government to raise revenue by any means, and, of course, it has been interpreted to include the right to tax in any number of ways. There are other sections of the Constitution which have been interpreted to buttress this position. Moreover, the right to tax has unfortunately been broadly interpreted to include the right to spend. Court interpretations have undermined the very basis of the federal principle, and have added to the acrimony in federal-provincial relations.

It is no wonder that Canadians are confused about who does what and when in their political institutions. Establishing and acknowledging a common identity as a people is even more problematic. A country cannot be built upon symbolic instruments such as the RCMP, the maple leaf flag, the beaver, hockey, etc. These are quite fragile and all, except the first, are certainly North American, rather than Canadian. Neither can it be built upon misguided notions of bi-culturalism between the English and the French, or upon multiculturalism.

These are false chimeras. An over emphasis on diversity, masquerading as tolerance and multiculturalism, has been a source of division rather than unity. Bankrolling cultural singularity creates permanent enclaves of difference and different living environments: islands of isolation. This cannot be a positive contributor to integration over time.

Canada's federal system is in a state of crisis. The Founders could have had no idea how the evolution of Canada's institutions would evolve. Their perspectives, as is usually the case, were temporal and contemporary to them. An East-West railway and high tariffs against US imports were intended to cement the country together. Instead, the federal system turned out to empower the provinces.Court decisions in the 1930s certainly buttressed the power of the provinces in the exercise of their constitutional responsibilities. While the intention of the founders was to have a fairly centralized federation, the outcome has been that Canada, arguably, is the most decentralized federation on the planet.

The spending power of the federal government is certainly the offset to growing provincial powers. Since this power has consistently been interpreted to include not only the power to tax, but also to spend in almost any way it sees fit, has been an unending source of conflict and confusion between the provinces and the federal government. The unceasing battles continue: the federal government wants a say in how its funds are spent in the provinces; the provinces want total control over program spending in areas of exclusive provincial jurisdiction, particularly in health and education.

Thousands of meetings at the officials', Assistant Deputy Minister, Deputy Minister, Ministers, and First Ministers levels since the 1940s has done little to ameliorate the tensions. Finance, Health, Education, Social Services, Labour, UN Conventions, etcetera, all involve coordination, and this is the raison d'être for the countless meetings at taxpayers' expense. It is always a shock when accommodations are actually forthcoming. Without a transfer of taxing powers to the provinces, the nation is in deep, deep trouble. There is no accountability, transparency or responsibility about who spends for what, when and how. It is an untenable system and is a major contributor to dysfunction in this country.

The unravelling of Canada is also obvious in what has become of its political institutions. Electing members to Parliament during elections should be an essential civic duty of all adults and it should mean something. Disappointingly, the House of Commons has become a laughable institution within the Commonwealth, unworthy of evolving British Parliamentary institutions and the very citizenry of this country. Except for the Cabinet, Members of Parliament have become mere mimics of whatever the PMO tells them to say and do. The forty-five minute question period, so essential to the peoples' understanding of the major and contemporary issues being considered, is a useless show that is usually uninformative and is contemptuous of all Canadians. Power is now fully in the hands of bureaucrats at the behest of the Prime Minister.

That backbenchers in **all** parties have not seized back their powers, based on the fair considerations of their constituents, is a condemning stain on Canada. How can a democracy be accepted and based upon a small cabal in Ottawa. MPs were never intended to be robots, based on the only principle of "everness": re-election and great pensions if one can get elected to a second term. MPs are elected to govern and definitely not to be puppets on a string. How embarrassing must this be domestically, and internationally, in terms of how others perceive this place. A system operating from the centre in this fashion undermines democracy and results in the general malaise and indifferent attitude towards Ottawa.

Moreover, it is unconceivable that the PMO could dictate votes and behaviour in the Senate but that is exactly what has happened in this country. Three Senators were forced to resign in late 2013, not due to internal operations and decisions of the Senate, but directed from the PMO. Whether the Prime Minister dictated decisions himself is almost irrelevant now. The point is that the Senate seems incapable of making any important decisions on its own. Far from being the chamber of "second sober thought", as originally intended, the Senate has become an institution of toadies, interested only in keeping their pensions intact. Perhaps Canadians should have always known that the Senate would not exactly be independent, given that all members are political appointees of the Prime Minister. Dysfunction from the outset leads to dysfunction in results!

A parliamentary system of government is based on the responsibility of the Cabinet to the House of Commons and, inter alia, the citizens of a country. Unelected Court appointees are now making decisions that have awesome and incredible impacts on the Canadian people. Decisions on taxing, such as the National Energy Program or the Goods and Services Tax, or abortion, First Nations' Rights, and, most recently, prostitution, have all undermined any reasonable concept of the Supremacy of Parliament. And this is a mere sampling of how the Supreme Court, in particular, has usurped the roles of duly elected MPs to rule this country.

There is no doubt that the reason that the Courts have been able to make final decisions in areas where they should not is because of a pusillanimous paralyzed Parliament that would rather leave things to the Courts rather than make democratic decisions based on informed, independent decisions and votes. Vacuums in politics always invite decisions in other places, whether they are appropriate or not. Courts are a backup mechanism; they are not, and have never been intended to be, principal decision-making devices. Political decisions made in Ottawa to relinquish the power of decision making in key moral areas undermines the very basis for a sustainable Canada.

Finally, the devastating foreign policy decisions of the Harper government will have a long lasting impact on how Canadians see themselves and how the international environment perceives this country. This country makes its foreign policy based on a deranged philosophy of "what is in it for us?" It took a generation and more to establish Canada as a middle power that values its status as a major contributor to peace and invests, with foreign aid, in so many countries with so little. Canada has been a peace-keeper, not a peace-maker, where it has been invited and encouraged to keep the peace, rather than make war.

In eight years, the current regime has undermined all concepts that have given Canada such a warm welcome in the international society of states. The country is seen now as a rogue state, a pariah. It is unfathomable that wearing the Canadian flag in foreign places would not bring smiles to peoples everywhere. No matter what future government is elected, reassembling the good will foreign policy of Canada will take many, many more years than the few it has taken to undo it.

The signs and the acts of successive Canadian governments, federal and provincial, have all contributed to the undoing of this experiment in democracy north of the US It is unclear what will happen in the future, and this book has not been an exercise in sorcery or clairvoyance. It has been an attempt to underline a few of the factors that are continuing to undermine the very basis of what Canadians, in general, think this country should be about. Carousel eight has stopped. What baggage will it deliver next?

Appendix 1

BC Health Care Premiums: Case Study

BC health care premiums are a case study in shame. BC, like all provinces, receives a significant amount of its funding for health care through the Canada Health Transfer (CHT). This is a block-funded program that originally was formulated in the halcyon days of cooperative federalism in 1976-77 and was named Established Programs Financing. It included funding for health care as well as post-secondary education. Shared-cost funding was replaced with this block fund which no longer was triggered by the amount a province spent; dollar for dollar funding was replaced with chunks of dollars with no conditions. About 27.6 percent of BC's health care expenditures in 2013-2014 will come from the federal government.

In 1984, the Trudeau government passed the Canada Health Act which included five conditions imposed on the provinces in order to qualify for a full entitlement of the yearly per capita amount. These conditions were a direct result of citizens' complaints about how the system was operating inequitably throughout Canada. The conditions are:

1. Universality (everyone in a province must be covered)
2. Accessibility (everyone must have reasonable access to the health system)
3. Comprehensiveness (services included must be broad)
4. Public Administration (services are to be provided through a central agency and doctors cannot collect from both the public and private sector simultaneously)
5. Portability (citizens can move from one province to any other and receive services)

Some provinces, including Alberta, attempted to circumvent these conditions through extra-billing charges for doctors' visits. Provinces engaging in these activities were penalized with dollar for dollar reductions in the amounts sent to them. Alberta was charged $35 million in one year.It was not the penalties that ultimately stopped provinces from extra-billing, but the sheer embarrassment of attempting to circumvent the public health care system, and putting more money in the hands of doctors. There was also an issue of accountability in that taxpayers were paying for a universal health care system but not getting their fair share of dollars back from it. Extra-billing $5 dollars per visit was quickly halted in Alberta, but not in BC

Only BC and Ontario currently require health care premiums to be paid by all citizens, except those falling below a certain net income. It is unclear and unfathomable why no federal government, Liberal or Conservative, has been challenged as to the constitutionality of such premiums based on Charter of Rights and Freedoms arguments.

The monthly required premium in BC is $66.50 for a single, $120.50 for two, and $133.30 for a family. These amounts rise every year, the latest for a single is about 4% even though wages and incomes have often fallen and many are living on part-time employment. This revenue grab should be investigated thoroughly.

These health care premiums are a tax, just like federal, provincial and sales taxes. Less money is in the taxpayer's pocket at the end of every month. Moreover, the health care premium tax discriminates. It discriminates against those in the private sector, students not covered and the retired. How does it do this? Many current public sector workers, private sector workers and union members are sheltered under a myriad of plans and are completely covered. Those not covered are left to their own devices to find the means to pay for coverage: No pay, no health care say, and likely, a very bad day!

What exactly happens to those that are not up to date with their BC health care premiums? Do they continue to receive health care services **equally** with all other residents that have had premiums paid for one way or another? No! Such permanent BC residents are unequally treated. Subsidies are available to those that fall below a certain net income threshold as established via the federal income tax system. This is nothing less than the US system of food stamps! In this case, it is effectively imaginary health stamps for coverage.

And what about those that do not qualify for a subsidy because of changed economic circumstances not evident in tax files? Well, they are welcome to call those that administer this reprehensible system in Victoria and plead their case. Whether they get to see their doctor or go to a medical clinic is at the mercy of ill-equipped administrative assistants. These folk are being asked to play economic, humanistic philosopher gods and goddesses. Shame on the BC Government for placing its employees in this situation!

Victoria's response to those that are in arrears in their health care premiums is to go to emergency. Surely, service is provided to all comers there. This is true, in a way. Services at emergency are triaged. Heart attacks, vehicle accidents, other very serious situations and conditions always come first, as is right. The problem is that this triaging can go on ceaselessly. An eight hour visit to emergency is not unheard of. Is this an appropriate use of the health care system? This manner of treating BC citizens is a travesty. It costs more for everyone, as a visit to a health care clinic is far less expensive to the health care system than a visit to the hospital.

This is where things get sinister. How does your local doctor or a health clinic know , first, that a person is not up to date with their health care premiums, and second, why would they care? The answer to the second question is easy: The doctor will not receive payment if the patient is in arrears. Their service would be gratis. And now doctors are uncomfortably being placed similarly as gods or goddesses to offer services without pay.

When entering a doctor's office with a legitimate BC health card, the following happens:

You are registered into the system;
You see the doctor;

The clerk bills the BC health care system;
The bill is paid

If the Medical Services plan fails to pay a medical bill, the following happens:

1. A message is generated saying, "Patient should phone MSP re: coverage or patient's coverage ended on "x" date". The systems used include Osler.
2. You are then billed by the doctor's office.
3. A note is placed in patient's file stating an invoice is payable.
4. If the invoice is not paid, the doctor decides whether you will be seen.
5. After three or so unpaid invoices, the bill is sent to collection. Doctors decide whether they will see patients for past unpaid visits.
6. If a person owes for past MSP payments, then several letters will be sent threatening collection activity.
7. A person can contact MSP and plead for a reduction in payments (payments are based on previous year's net income).
8. If no payments are received, Revenue Canada is then notified and can and will collect premiums on behalf of the province; refunds, Child Tax benefits, student credits etc. can all be rebated back to the province from individual.
9. Anyone leaving the province and coming back without paying back amounts owed will not be re-instated, thus denying any access to the B.C health care system.

There are a number of serious issues that need to be addressed here:

1. Medical Office Assistants (MOAs) and doctors are receiving personal information from Victoria about clients' payment histories. Access to such information violates privacy and clearly raises Charter of Rights issues.

2. Citizens in BC are being denied basic services for failure to pay premiums (emergency rooms do not provide routine physicals for obvious reasons, as an example).
3. Portability is being denied to those BC citizens returning with past premium issues.
4. Universality is being denied to persons in arrears as they simply are not covered except at emergency.
5. Accessibility is being denied, as it is only available at emergency.
6. Comprehensiveness is clearly negated as basic services available at a clinic or doctor's office are denied.
7. Public Administration is undermined and confidence in the health care system decimated with the interplay of information provided from Victoria and tax refunds withdrawn from citizens and re-directed to Victoria's coffers.

What this case study demonstrates clearly is a basic demeaning of the entire health care system in BC doctors have access to information that is outside their interests. They are playing gods and goddesses as to who gets service. Those providing the information are in complicity. The privacy issues here alone could provide generations of lawyers with Charter work!

All five of the conditions of the Canada Health Act are being blatantly violated. The federal government is turning its head and continuing to pay the province its per capita entitlement.

As for the dysfunctional nature of federalism in Canada, the issue is obvious: Ottawa is playing handmaiden to the province of BC in collecting a myriad of tax refund entitlements due citizens and remitting them back to the province. There is no law providing for such collection. What regulatory statutes are being used or abused to provide for such activity? What are the underlying ideological motives for such collection? Inter-delegation of constitutional responsibilities would seem to be clearly unconstitutional. In any event, it is not surprising that BC citizens affected by what has happened to them are confused as to who is responsible for what. When the appropriate government cannot be held responsible, government is eroded, and the entire federal system brought into question.

If the federal government is prepared to collect back payments of unpaid health care premiums in BC, then what prevents them from collecting owed property taxes, consumer debt, or anything else perceived to be owing? The point of this mini-case study is to demonstrate the dysfunctional nature of a federal system which treats citizens differently from province to province, engages in unconstitutional activities, and undermines any basic commitment of accountability to citizens. What has happened to the basic democratic principle of responsible government? Maybe George Orwell had it right: Big brother is already here. Shame on BC, and shame on Ottawa!

Appendix 2

Harper and Ford: Emperors with Their Pants Down?

There is no doubt that the antics of Mayor Rob Ford in 2013 have put Canada on the world map of comedy for many, many years. "Ford Nation" makes "Colbert Nation" look like girl scouts baking cookies. All of the major late night US entertainment shows in November and December 2013 were given a plethora of outrageously comical material to cull from Toronto's silly house that they call City Council. CNN picked up on the fun and it is a guarantee that their ratings skyrocketed. The latest buffoonery emanating from Ford tops anything that media can paste on TV: not the unending Edward Snowden revelations about the activities of the US National Security Agency; not the latest school shootings in Littleton, Colorado; not the unending battles in the US Congress over budgets.

    The Canadian reaction has been a bit more subdued. Nonetheless, the RCMP released tape (with perhaps more to come) is damning evidence of some of the potential illegal antics of Ford. Urinating in public places, waddling around in a perceived drunken state, and smoking something like crack cocaine with strange characters is behaviour unbecoming of someone that rules the largest and most prestigious city in Canada. Even Canadians have had to shake their heads, wake up and take notice.

    That Ford has confessed to smoking crack cocaine and drinking and driving adds fuel to the fire. His behaviour within city council has not helped his case. From mocking another counsellor with arm motions about drinking to bowling over a fellow councillor while trying to attack a heckler attending the proceedings. Inferring that a Toronto Star reporter is a pedophile, pseudo apologizing, and still incurring a civil law suit adds to the mix. It is little wonder that the Toronto City

Council of forty-five has relieved Mayor Ford of his duties until further notice. Somehow he thinks that "Ford Nation" supporters in both the urban and suburban areas of Toronto will vindicate him in the next political elector cycle in 2014. That may very well depend on whether he is charged and convicted of any criminal behavior in the interim. What kind of signals does this politician send to citizens within this country? More importantly, how are children to comprehend such activities? His comment in Council quarters regarding what he "eats" in the sexual sense with whom, and what he does, and how he may or may not service his wife are really beyond the pale of civility. Half-apologies here and there do not count; the mea culpa strategy has not stopped the bullying. What kind of kid in school was Rob Ford, or his brother Doug, for that matter? Surely they were to be feared rather than loved! This is indeed an emperor caught with his pants down.

And what about the Grand Emperor, Prime Minister Stephen Harper? Where Mayor Ford is all about the cult of personality, Harper is all about the cult of unilateral deliverance. Power is perhaps the ultimate aphrodisiac in politics. There is a reason for the quote: Power corrupts, and absolute power corrupts absolutely. The only thing saving Canada is that it remains a democratic country and the elections come around every four years or so.

What has given Harper so much power is a political system based on majority rule in the Parliament. Whoever has that majority can carry an iron stick and push through whatever agenda it wants. Majority rule certainly has a nice resonance to it. The problem is that the Canadian Parliamentary system no longer capable of respecting the concept of "responsible government," whereby the appointed members to the Cabinet are responsible to their party members and, indirectly, to all members of Parliament. The power of the Prime Minister's Office and now the Privy Council Office are directing the regulatory and legislative schedule and back benchers have been relegated to the sidelines; puppets on a string. What this has done is to give the Prime Minister the power of a king.

Harper's political behavior is motivated by both ideology and getting re-elected. His opposition to legalization of marijuana, tougher mandatory sentences for criminal activity, and opposition to the long gun registry are examples of the ideology. Opposition to expansion of the Canada Pension Plan for the many that have falling living standards is another. He has shied from entering the abortion issue, but seems firmly opposed to "dying with dignity" issues. Keeping a close tap on the electorate is his mantra.

What is getting Harper into perpetual trouble is the Senate scandal. Who knew what and when? How many people in the PMO were aware of what kinds of deals were made with Senator Duffy? Was Nigel Wright, his Chief of Staff, solely responsible for the $90,000 payment to Duffy to pay off illegally claimed expenses? What would provoke such an act of beneficence? Why would the Prime Minister throw him to the wolves, as he was his principal advisor? Is it really possible that the Prime Minister knew nothing about what the minions were doing in the PMO? Either way, Harper is "up a creek." If he knew what was going on, he should have resigned. If he didn't know, then he has no control over his most trusted offices. And he should resign because "the buck," as President Truman was fond of saying, stops at the Oval Office. The Prime Minister has been caught with his pants down, and other democratic, parliamentary systems would have demanded a resignation. Opposition NDP leader Mulcair has done his part in asking the tough questions for which the Conservatives have absolutely no believable answers. Perhaps Harper thinks that the 2015 election is far enough away that he can weather this storm and emerge for the Conservatives to win yet another election. Stranger things have happened in recent Canadian electoral history: consider the Christy Clarke shocker in BC and the Alison Redford surprise in Alberta.

What do Rob Ford and Stephen Harper have in common? Two things: First, they both share a basic conservative philosophy of deficit control and Ford continues to be useful to Harper, as he can still deliver electoral MP seats in the greater Toronto region. Second, they both have been caught with their pants down! Though their personalities are quite different: Ford is the boisterous, outgoing bullying clown; Harper the ultimate calculating Machiavellian type. The result is the same, although the consequences for Canada, its institutions, the future of federal-provincial relations, and of Canada's place in the world are absolutely being bruised and undermined by the unilateral activities and musings of this Prime Minister since his 2006 occupancy of the office. This appendix illustrates a Canada in decline.

Notes

Chapter one (Introduction)

1. https://www.youtube.com/watch?v=zIEIvi2MuEk, Dec 9, 2013

2. Tumulty, Karen, "American Exceptionalism Explained." Wash. Post, Sept. 12, 2013.

4. As quoted at www.ctvnews.ca/ Aug. 29, 2013.

op. cit. youtube.com

5. Morgentaler v. the Queen {1976} 1 S.C.R. 616

6. Canada v. Bedford {2013} S.C.C. 72

7. http://www. pco-bcp.gc.ca/aia/index/asp?Lang=eng

8. http://mapleleafweb.com/features/Charlottetown-accord-history-and-0

Chapter two: Canadian Political Identity

1. Raney, Tracy, cpsa-acsp.ca/paper 2004, p.5

2. http://www.literature.org/authors/Carroll-Lewis/alices-adventures-in-wonderland.

3. http://www.filibustercartoons.com/greatest%Canadians.html

4. http://www.google.ca//#q=Norway+Maple+Leafs+Ont+20+dollar+bill

5. http://www.britannica.com/EBchecked/topic/505847/roc

6. op.cit. Raney, p.23

7. Henderson, Ailsa, CJPS37(2004) p.607

8. Ignatieff, Peter, True Patriot Love: Four Generations in Search of Canada, Penguin, 2012

9. http:www.amazon.ca/no-exit-three other plays/dp/0679725164

Chapter Three: Multiculturalism: Diversity, Inclusion and the Limits of Tolerance

1. As quoted by Taber and Mackrael, Globe and Mail, Aug 29. , 2013

2. Kymlicka, Will, "The 3 lives of Multiculturalism," UBC-Laurier Institute Multiculturalism Lecture, April 2008

3. Hogg, Peter, Constitutional Law of Canada, Toronto: Carswell, (1982)

4. http://www.pbs-clcc.gc.ca/infocntr/multi-eng.shtml

5. Gregg, Allen, Walrus, March 2006

6. Banting et. al., Belonging? Diversity, Recognition and Shared Citizenship in Canada, 2007, p. 649

7. Taylor, Charles, Multiculturalism: Examining The Politics of Recognition, 1994, p. 26

8. Moynihan, Daniel, Beyond the Melting Pot, MIT Press, 2nd. ed. , 1970

9. Donnelly, Jack, "The Relative Universality of Human Rights," Human Rights Quarterly, vol. 29, No.2, 2007

10. Donnelly, Jack, Universal Human Rights in Theory and Practice, Cornell Univ. Press, 2013

11. Berlin, I., "Two Concepts of Liberty," in Berlin, Four Essays on Liberty, Oxford Univ. Press, 2002

12. Rawls, John, A Theory of Justice, Harvard Univ. Press, 1971

13. Blaikie, Peter, Dissertation, Univ. of Alberta, 1977

14. See Nozick, R. Anarchy, State and Utopia, Basic Books, 1974

15. Putnam, Robert, "E Pluribus Unum: Diversity and Community in the 21 First Century", Scandinavian Political Studies, June, 2007

16. Bill 60, Govt. of Quebec, 2013

17. Rand, David, "Why a Secular Charter is Good for Quebec," Globe and Mail, Sept. 10, 2013

18. Locke, John, "A Letter Concerning Toleration," James Tully(ed.) Indianapolis: Hackett Publishing, 1983

19. Rousseau, J.J., The Social Contract and Discourses, London and Toronto: J.M. Dent and Sons, 1923

20. Hobbes, Thomas, Leviathan, Univ. of Oregon Press, 1999

21. ibid. ch. 13

Chapter Four: The Federal Spending Power

1. A.G. Canada v. A.G. Ontario {1937}. A. C. 355-356

2. www.pco-bcp.gc.ca/aia

3. Brouillet, Eugenie, SCLR (2006) 34 2nd. ed. ,p.313

4. ibid, p. 319

5. Belanger, Claude, Canadian Federalism, The Tax Rental Agreements of the Period 1941-62 and Fiscal Federalism from 1962-77, Quebec History, 2001

6. Brouillet, op. cit. p. 309

7. Finlay v. Canada {1986} 2 S.C.R., 607

8. Reference re: Canada Assistance Plan (BC) 1991, 2 S.C.R. p. 525

9. ibid. p. 529

10. ibid. p.530

11. ibid. p. 529

12. Winterhaven Stables Ltd. v. Canada (A.G.), 1988

13. Richer, Karen, http://www.parl.gc.ca./content,2007

14. Winterhaven Stables Ltd. v. Canada (1988) 53 Dominion Law Reports (4th series) 413

15. Edwards v. Canada (A.G.), 1929

16 Reference re: Same Sex Marriage (2004) S.C.P. 698

17. Haas, Ernest, The Uniting of Europe, Stanford Univ. Press, 1956

18. Reference re: Secession of Quebec {1987} 2 S.C.R. 217

19. Telford, Hamish, "The Federal Spending Power in Canada: Nation Building or Nation Destroying," Publius: The Journal of Federalism 33 Winter 2003, p. 6

20. Quoted in Telford, Hamish, IRPP Policy Matters, Sept. 2008

21. Hogg, Peter, Constitutional Law of Canada, 2nd. ed. Toronto: Carswell Company, 1985, p. 124

22. Hogg, Peter, Constitutional Law of Canada, 4th. ed. Toronto: Carswell Company, 1997, pp 17-18

23. Verrelli, Nadia, "The Federal Spending Power,"Working paper 2008, IRRP, Queens Univ, p. 13

24. www.pco-bcp.gc.ca, Jan. 28, 1999, Dion, Stephen, Notes for an address to students at U. of Toronto

25. http://www. parl. gc.ca/Parlinfo/Documents/Throne Speech/39-2-e.html

26. op. cit. As quoted in Telford, Hamish, Conference of Federal and Provincial Governments, 1955, p. 36

27. idid, p. 38

28. Annual Premier's Conference, 1984

29. Leslie, Peter(ed.), Canada, The State of the Federation, Institute of Intergov. Relations, Queens Univ., p.10

30. Belanger-Campeau Commission on the Political and Constitutional Future of Quebec, 1991, p. 48

31. www.saic.gouv.qc.ca/publications/documents_inst/positionEng.pdf

32. Govt. of Alberta Discussion Paper, Alberta in Canada: Strength in Diversity, 1983

33. www.cpac.ca/en/1999-united-alternative-national convention

34. Adam, Marc-Antoine, Policy Options, Mar. 2007

35. Govt. of Canada, Social Union: "A Framework to Improve the Social Union For Canadians: An Agreement Between the Govt. of Canada and the Govt's of the Provinces and Territories, Feb. 1999

36. http//www. mondopolitico.com/library/myth/ sec3, p.2 html

37. ibid. sec 3, p. 3

Chapter Five: Institutions

1. As quoted by Ibbitson, John, Globe and Mail, Feb. 2, 2013

2. As reported by Mackrael, Kim, Globe and Mail, Dec. 3, 2012

3. The term was coined by Preston Manning and the Reform Party

4. Dicey, A.V., Introduction to the Study of the Law of the Constitution, 8th ed. 1915 (Liberty Classic, 1982) pp 3. 4

5. Canada (A.G) v. Bedford, 2013

6. Moore v. British Columbia Education, SCC61, 2012

Chapter Six: Intergovernmental Situations

1. Savoie, Donald, Globe and Mail, June 29, 2012

2. See the Constitution Act, 1982, s. 33

3. As quoted by Ivison, John, National Post, June 28, 2012

4. The term was used as early as 1970 by Quebec Premier Bourassa

5. See Rand, Ayn, Atlas Shrugged, (1992), N.Y.: Dutton, Originally published in 1957

6. As published in the National Post, Jan. 24, 2001

7. www.NewWestPartnershipTrade.ca

8. www.theglobeand mail.com/news/opinions, May 1, 2010

9. Mendelsohn, Matthew, http://mowatcentre.ca/wp-content/uploads/publications/58/back_to_basics_future.pdf, p.16

10. ibid. p. 8

11. ibid. p. 10

Chapter Seven: Federal-Provincial Fiscal Transfer Relations

1. Courchene, Tom, Policy Options, May 2010, p. 38

2. Fin.gc.ca/fedprov/mtp-eng.asp

3. BC Budget Papers, Report G, CHST, 1997

4. Courchene, Tom, "Reflections on the Federal Spending Power," IRPP Working Paper, June 2008, p. 16

5. Council of the Federation, May 2005

6. report_fiscalim_mar3106. pdf : Reconciling the Irreconcilable, Addressing Canada's Fiscal Imbalance, Advisory Committee on Fiscal Imbalance, 2006

7. ibid. p.32

8. Mendelson, Michael, "Is Canada (still) a Fiscal Union," Caledon Institute of Social Policy, 2012, p.12

9. Lasswell, Harold, Politics: Who Gets What, When, How, McGraw-Hill, 1936

Chapter Eight: Canadian Foreign Policy

1. Nye, Joseph,"Soft Power: The Means to Success in World Politics," Public Affairs, 2004

2. Clausewitz, Carl von, On War, www.clausewitz.com/readings/ONWAR1873/Toc.htm

3. http://alberta views/ab.ca/wp-content/uploads

4. http://www.international.gc.ca/media/comm/news-communiqueé2013/11/27a.aspx?lang=,p.2

5. ibid. p.1

6. http//www.Canadainternational.gc.ca/prmny-mponu/Canada_unCanada

7. CBC.ca, Dec. 13, 2011

8. Globe and Mail, Mar. 28, 2013

9. Austin Powers: The Spy Who Shagged Me, www.imdb.com/title/tt0145660